BRITISH AUTHORS

Introductory Critical Studies

General Editor: ROBIN MAYHEAD

WILLIAM WORDSWORTH

In this series

John Keats by ROBIN MAYHEAD

WILLIAM WORDSWORTH

BY

GEOFFREY DURRANT

Professor of English Literature
University of British Columbia
Vancouver

CAMBRIDGE

AT THE UNIVERSITY PRESS

1969

Published by the Syndics of the Cambridge University Press
Bentley House, 200 Euston Road, London N.W.1
American Branch: 32 East 57th Street, New York, N.Y. 10022

Library of Congress Catalogue Card Number: 70–79054/
Standard Book Number: 521 07608 0   √

Printed in Great Britain by
Alden & Mowbray Ltd
at the Alden Press, Oxford

GENERAL PREFACE

This study of Wordsworth is the second in a series of short introductory critical studies of the more important British authors. The aim of the series is to go straight to the authors' works; to discuss them directly with a maximum of attention to concrete detail; to say what they are and what they do, and to indicate a valuation. The general critical attitude implied in the series is set out at some length in my *Understanding Literature*. Great literature is taken to be to a large extent self-explanatory to the reader who will attend carefully enough to what it says. 'Background' study, whether biographical or historical, is not the concern of the series.

It is hoped that this approach will suit a number of kinds of reader, in particular the general reader who would like an introduction which talks about the works themselves; and the student who would like a general critical study as a starting point, intending to go on to read more specialized works later. Since 'background' is not erected as an insuperable obstacle, readers in other English-speaking countries, countries where English is a second language, or even those for whom English is a foreign language, should find the books helpful. In Britain and the Commonwealth, students and teachers in universities and in the higher forms of secondary schools will find that the authors chosen for treatment are those most often prescribed for study in public and university examinations.

The series could be described as an attempt to make available to a wide public the results of the literary criticism of the last thirty years, and especially the methods associated with Cambridge. If the result is an increase in the reading, with enjoyment and understanding, of the great works of English literature, the books will have fulfilled their wider purpose.

ROBIN MAYHEAD

CONTENTS

The quotations from Wordsworth's poems, and the variant readings, are from *Wordsworth's Poetical Works*, edited by Ernest de Selincourt and Helen Darbishire, five volumes, Oxford University Press, 1940–9 and from *Wordsworth's Prelude*, edited by Ernest de Selincourt and revised by Helen Darbishire, Oxford University Press, 1959

INTRODUCTORY

An introduction to a poet whose work extends over a period of fifty years must either attempt a general survey, or concentrate on individual poems in an attempt to show something of the range and quality of the achievement. I have chosen the second method, partly because there are other introductory studies that offer a general survey, but chiefly because experience has shown that readers of Wordsworth at first pass too lightly over poems that require for full understanding the close attention that Wordsworth himself insisted was necessary. Of a reader who remarked on the pleasure given by the poem on 'daffodils reflected in the water' he observed that the poem must have been carelessly read: 'My poems must be more nearly looked at before they can give rise to remarks of much value, even from the strongest minds.' When more nearly looked at, Wordsworth's poems reveal qualities of imagination and intelligence that may not be suspected at a first reading; they also show a poetic integrity which affords a deeper pleasure with each new reading. With this in mind, I have concentrated in this study on a number of major poems of the period from 1798 to 1805, when Wordsworth's powers were at their height, and when his best work was written. The earlier work is experiment and preparation, the later work a slow falling-off into a less intense and vital mode.

The poems of 1798–1805 have a vitality which springs from a struggle of the mind to come to terms with the situation of man in a world transformed by the progress of natural science. The view offered by classical poetry and philosophy, and by traditional religion, was of a world in which man himself, whatever his sufferings, was a being of special importance, unique and with an immortal soul. Though this view had been challenged often enough before, the completeness of the view of the world offered at the end of the eighteenth century by natural science seemed at last to be destroying the very concept of man as a uniquely valuable creature. If every event in the world and even in the mind of man can ultimately be explained by natural laws it seems that man himself is a fleeting consciousness imprisoned in the body, and doomed to extinction when the body dissolves. Modern man has perhaps come to terms with this view; if so, it is partly because such imaginative minds as Wordsworth's have ventured boldly into a new and unfamiliar world of thought. Wordsworth had the courage to follow in the footsteps of the man of science, and to imagine a world in which man is finally alone, and in which he faces certain extinction. There is, however, nothing depressing or morbid in this vision; on the contrary, the challenge is invigorating, the delight in unclouded perception is keen, and the dominant mood is of a calm suffused with joy.

The problem for Wordsworth was to come to terms with what seemed to him to be the facts of the universe, without accepting a bleakly mechanistic view of the world and of man's place in it. Solitude is a recurrent theme in Wordsworth's poetry; the task of the poet was to transform the desolation of mere loneliness into the 'bliss of solitude'—that 'blessed mood' in which the human mind irradiates and transforms the world which it perceives, giving life and meaning to what otherwise would be essentially dead. It is the poet who most often achieves this transformation. Many of Wordsworth's poems are about the poet, either explicitly or by implication, because for Wordsworth the poetic power was the saving grace through which all men could in varying degrees be rescued from the 'visionary dreariness' of a life without joy. Since men could no longer look to the gods or angels to work miracles for them, they must work their own miracles of the mind. The poet, as 'a man speaking to men', was one who had devoted his whole life to this task; he was to be the guide and leader of his fellow-men in their search for a mode of experience that would transform the world without falsifying it. This task involved a courageous clear-sightedness, and a thorough-going overhaul of the language of poetry as the instrument of a new mode of perception.

Wordsworth records in *The Prelude* and in *The Excursion* the activity of a young mind actively transforming the world, investing the objects of sense with a 'glory not their own'. The classical poets whom Wordsworth loved from boyhood made no sharp division between the human spirit and the divine. Gods put on mortal garb and became men, and men might become god-like. Nature itself was subject to the same transformations. A hyacinth, a reed by the river, a laurel bush, a constellation, were all the visible expressions of the interaction of the natural and the divine. The human spirit knew no limitations, whatever indignities the body might have to accept. Death itself set no limits to the mind, since death was only a change of state, the human soul entering a new condition in the stars, in the underworld, or in a new existence. Wordsworth's youthful imagination, nourished on the poetry of the ancient world, similarly transformed the natural scene, investing it with terror and delight. As he rows on the lake in a borrowed boat, the young poet's slight sense of guilt transforms the mountain into an avenging giant towering over him, so that it fills his dreams for many nights. The valleys of Westmorland were seen in the light of ancient poetry:

> An auxiliar light
> Came from my mind, which on the setting sun
> Bestowed new splendour; the melodious birds,
> The fluttering breezes, fountains that run on
> Murmuring so sweetly in themselves, obeyed
> A like dominion, and the midnight storm
> Grew darker in the presence of my eye.
> (*The Prelude*, II, 368–74)

There is nothing unfamiliar in this. All young minds have this capacity—what Wordsworth calls 'a plastic power'—to give life and meaning to the commonplace, to cast over it 'the consecration and the poet's dream'. The boy who on his way to school sees himself as an explorer of space or of the Brazilian jungle is engaged in a similar poetic activity. The source of such daydreaming is always to be found in imaginative experience gained from stories, books, or the drama. Nor is this a peculiar habit of 'romantic' poets. All poets from Homer onwards have achieved a similar imaginative transformation of the world of common sense.

3

For most of us, the process of growing up and of becoming 'serious' involves the loss of this habit, if we are not to live as Walter Mittys. It is the poet's task to preserve the habit, the 'plastic power', while uniting it with a coherent and adult view of the world.

The task of preserving the visionary power without sacrifice of seriousness and of truth was a supreme challenge to Wordsworth, since far more than most poets he knew and respected the laws of nature, which no imaginative colourings can change. His education at school and at Cambridge was in Latin poetry and in mathematics, and much of his poetry depends on the struggle to reconcile the two. The poetry of the ancient world strengthened his belief in the power of the human mind to transform reality; the poet, as a votary of Apollo, could create a world of joy:

> His fancy fetched,
> Even from the blazing chariot of the sun,
> A beardless Youth, who touched a golden lute,
> And filled the illumined groves with ravishment.
>
> (*The Excursion*, IV, 857–60)

On the other hand Wordsworth's education in mathematics confronted him with an aspect of reality utterly resistant to the transforming power of the mind. As Housman puts it:

> To think that two and two are four
> And neither five nor three
> The heart of man has long been sore
> And long 'tis like to be.

Mathematics in Cambridge, in Wordsworth's day, included astronomy, and above all the study of Newton. Newton's *Principia Mathematica* had presented for the first time an account of the physical universe in which all observable movements could be described in mathematical terms, and reduced to a few simple laws. The movement of a stone thrown by a schoolboy, and the movements of the stars and planets, formed parts of a single system. This system was so complete that it seemed to be self-contained and self-perpetuating. Nothing, least of all the puny thoughts of an individual mind, could disturb its majestic order. In spite of changes in scientific theory, and the newer ideas of relativity and indeterminacy, the universe as modern man imagines it is the universe of Newton—an infinity of space in which inert masses are moved by the operation of absolute law. It was Wordsworth's self-imposed task to achieve a poetic vision which respected this order, which celebrated its grandeur and beauty, without reducing the human mind itself to nothingness. Consequently the poems of the great period are concerned principally with two inter-connected themes—the place of man in the physical universe, and the power of the human mind to transform within certain limits the conditions of its own existence. The 'Lucy' poems and the 'Matthew' poems, for example, define the limits of human existence. The girl and the old man are loved and valued; but no love or friendship, no desire or fancy of the poet's, can do anything to change the laws that govern their fate. Within these limits, however, man can achieve a certain independence; he can transform the prison-house of natural law into a place of joy. In 'I wandered lonely as a cloud' a mind that has been trained to this activity—the mind of a poet—is shown delighting in the complex patterns of the physical universe, seeing the dance of the flowers in the wind as akin to the dance of the waves, the arrangement of the daffodils along the shore of the lake as related to the curve of the stars in the galaxy. In this way the world is transformed but not falsified.

This then is the task undertaken by Wordsworth, and achieved during the great period—the transformation of the world without sacrifice of truth. The aim is stated in the 1800 Preface to *Lyrical Ballads*:

The Man of Science seeks truth as a remote and unknown benefactor; he cherishes and loves it in his solitude: the Poet, singing a song in which all human beings join with him, rejoices in the presence of truth as our visible friend and hourly companion.

Wordsworth is not advancing a theory of 'poetic truth'; there is for him no difference between the 'truth' of the man of science and the 'truth' of the poet. There is only one kind of truth, although there is more than one way of pursuing it, and more than one way of communicating it. The poet experiences the world and its truths as an individual person, and he speaks to others not as a specialist, but as 'a man speaking to men'.

The poems of the great period involve an intense activity of mind. Wordsworth is engaged in the task of giving human significance and life to a world which in its main outline has already been explored and charted by the scientist. Blake rejected science:

> The Atoms of Democritus
> And Newton's Particles of light
> Are sands upon the Red Sea shore
> Where Israel's tents do shine so bright.

Keats exclaimed against the deadening effect of 'cold Philosophy', by which he meant science. Wordsworth, in spite of his hostility to the moral science of his day (which we should call psychology and sociology), looked with the deepest respect on the work of Newton, and did not dream of challenging the authority of the physical sciences. On the contrary, the scientific view of the universe, as I shall try to show, is interwoven into the pattern of his thought.

The danger of this acceptance of the scientific view of the world is that it may in the end take the place of poetic exploration. In the 'Ode to Duty' (1804) the natural laws are shown as requiring a somewhat passive assent; men perhaps ought to submit themselves to authority, as natural objects—flowers and stars—are seen to do:

> Stern Lawgiver! yet dost thou wear
> The Godhead's most benignant grace;
> Nor know we anything so fair
> As is the smile upon thy face:
> Flowers laugh before thee on their beds
> And fragrance in thy footing treads;
> Thou dost preserve the stars from wrong;
> And the most ancient heavens, through Thee, are fresh and strong.

This poem reveals some distrust of the poet's own moral judgment, and perhaps the beginnings of a weariness with the poet's task. 'The genial sense of youth' upon which Wordsworth had relied seemed no longer a secure guide, and he had begun to long for 'a repose that ever is the same'. This weariness, and the accompanying love of a settled life, and of an established social and moral order, produced the poetry of the later years—a poetry in which there are occasional quickenings of the former intellectual life, but which for the most part has settled into a more diffuse philosophizing. The conservative opinions and the orthodox religious views of Wordsworth's later years may be taken as an expression of a love of order which cannot be dissociated from a certain exhaustion. There was no deep conviction in Wordsworth's Toryism or in his Anglicanism; the acceptance of the natural order in the universe seems to have led him to the acceptance of the established order in Church and State. In the poems we are to study, however, the natural order is by no means an entirely benignant power. Though it is the creator and preserver, it is also the destroyer of human hopes and human lives. Wordsworth seeks out the principle of joy wherever it can be found, but does not shrink from the contemplation of the ultimate nothingness. Still less is there any morbid or sensationalist cultivation of misery and despair; Wordsworth's genius is marked by an unusual degree of good sense and robust moral health. When he confronts a painful truth, we feel that he does so for the sake of the truth, and not for the emotional stimulus of the pain.

There is a natural tendency to seek in the work of a 'romantic' poet for the emotional intensities. These are to be found in Wordsworth's work, especially when he is dramatically representing human emotion. So a mother's grief for a lost son is given a poignant expression:

> Perhaps some dungeon hears thee groan,
> Maimed, mangled by inhuman men;
> Or thou upon a desert thrown
> Inheritest the lion's den;
> Or hast been summoned to the deep,
> Thou, thou, and all thy mates, to keep
> An incommunicable sleep.
>
> ('The Affliction of Margaret', 1804)

Here the grief is moderated by the elegiac manner, and by the suggestion of a common and inescapable fate in 'Thou, thou, and all thy mates'. The mother feels not only a personal grief for her son, but grief for other men lost in the anonymity of death. In 'Resolution and Independence' the poet's fears for himself are generalized; what begins as personal anxiety—as fear of 'Solitude, pain of heart, distress, and poverty'—becomes a part of an account of the fate of all men, and especially of poets:

> Cold, pain, and labour, and all fleshly ills;
> And mighty Poets in their misery dead.

Even at its most 'romantic', Wordsworth's poetry is elegiac, contemplative, and philosophical, rather than simple, sensuous, and passionate. The highland girl singing 'a melancholy strain' as she reaps alone in the field expresses for the poet not a personal feeling, but a melancholy suffused over vast areas of space and time, a song of the common fate of men not only in battle but also in the more ordinary affairs of daily life.

> Perhaps the plaintive numbers flow
> For old, unhappy, far-off things,
> And battles long ago:
> Or is it some more humble lay,
> Familiar matter of today?
> Some natural sorrow, loss, or pain,
> That has been, and may be again.
>
> ('The Solitary Reaper', 1805)

Here again the consciousness of human unhappiness is controlled by a quiet recognition that sorrow is natural, that it will recur, and that all is bearable when it is sung of by the poet or the highland girl. In this way Wordsworth achieves a 'distancing' of the emotions he describes.

Some misunderstanding has been caused by frequent quotation —sometimes out of context—of such phrases as 'emotion recollected in tranquillity', and 'poetry is the spontaneous overflow of powerful feelings'. Elsewhere in the Preface to the 1800 edition of *Lyrical Ballads* Wordsworth shows that he regards poetry as a mode of thought, as a *considering* of a man's condition in the world. The distinction he makes between poetry and science is not between opposites or enemies, but between allies which work to the same end, but use different methods. The 'man of science' is a specialist isolated from other men, and using a language strange to them; the poet, though like the man of science he seeks the pleasure of knowledge, must not lose touch with his fellow-men, but must use a language they can understand. The experiment with simple language represents Wordsworth's determination to carry out this task. It was, however, no part of Wordsworth's poetic aim to unite his readers in the communion of simple and intense emotions. The pleasure to be given by his poetry was to be the pleasure of knowledge. Aristotle explains the pleasure given by works of art by remarking that all men enjoy imitation, because by imitation we 'learn the nature of things'. This is Wordsworth's general position, both in theory and in his poetic practice. The pleasure given by his poetry is essentially that of having been shown something, made to see what one could not see without his help.

This is of course not to assert that his poetry is without passion. On the contrary, the more intense the contemplation and the more precise an expression is given to it, the deeper runs the current of poetic passion. The most usual mode of feeling associated with Wordsworth's poetry is a mixture of intellectual excitement and gratification—excitement aroused by the poet's sure insight, and gratification caused by the authoritative art which makes this insight available to us in words so unerringly chosen. Here for example is a representation of a boy's sense of guilt when he has broken down the branches of a hazel to gather nuts:

> Then up I rose
> And dragged to earth both branch and bough, with crash
> And merciless ravage; and the shady nook
> Of hazels, and the green and mossy bower,
> Deformed and sullied, patiently gave up
> Their quiet being.

('Nutting', 1798)

The physical act is vividly represented here by the violent regularity of the second line, with its recurrent harsh initial consonants. The boy's exultation in his triumph is tinged, as all such experience is, with a sense of awe and of regret; something has been destroyed by his act, and with it part of himself is lost. The bower is surprisingly said to be 'deformed and sullied';

the effect is to suggest that the boy himself has been betrayed by his act. The incident is deliberately given the quality of a rape, in which the violator suffers as much as the violated. The association of bowers, gardens, and valleys with sexuality is traditional in Western poetry, and Wordsworth himself makes use of it in a poem written at the age of sixteen:

> Let thy softest pencil throw
> O'er her neck a tint of snow,
> There let all the Loves repair,
> Let all the Graces flutter there.
> Loosely chaste o'er all below
> Let the snowy mantle flow,
> As silvered by the morning beam
> The white mist curls on Grasmere's stream,
> Which like a veil of flowing light
> Hides half the landskip from the sight.
> Here I see the wandering rill,
> The white flocks seated on the hill,
> While Fancy paints, beneath the veil,
> The pathway winding through the dale,
> The cot, the seat of Peace and Love,
> Peeping through the tufted grove.
>
> ('Anacreon', 1786)

The deliberate sexuality of the passage from 'Nutting' makes what would otherwise be a mere biographical anecdote into a representation of a universal human experience—the realization that, as Wordsworth himself expressed it in 'The Borderers':

> Action is transitory—a step, a blow,
> The motion of a muscle—this way or that—
> 'Tis done, and in the after-vacancy
> We wonder at ourselves like men betrayed.
>
> (Act III, 1539–42)

The pleasure offered by 'Nutting' is that of delighted recognition of our own experience, made intelligible and given permanent expression by the poet's art.

Because Wordsworth sometimes achieves broad and simple effects, it is often assumed that he is to be read by general impression, and that close attention to detail would be a murdering to dissect. Certainly there is something to be enjoyed in Wordsworth if he is read by general impression, but only the most alert attention to the actual words of the poems can enable the reader to respond to them fully. In 'A slumber did my spirit seal' Lucy is said, after her death, to be

> Rolled round in earth's diurnal course
> With rocks, and stones, and trees.

Here 'diurnal' is placed among common English words. As a technical term in astronomy, it compels the reader to imagine the movement of the earth in the context of the whole universe, so that part of the experience described is the sense of the vastness of the system into which Lucy's life is absorbed. The very smallest turns of phrase often carry a considerable load of meaning. When, in 'I wandered lonely as a cloud', Wordsworth declares that 'a poet could not but be gay' he is not merely saying rather clumsily that the daffodils made him happy. He is asserting a view more fully advanced in the Preface to *Lyrical Ballads*—that a poet is a man who has so trained his senses and his imagination that he responds spontaneously and almost automatically to an experience which for other men might be meaningless.

Sometimes the verbal life is manifested in humour and allusion. When the poet begins to tell the story of Peter Bell, he starts in a solemn epic style (191–5):

> All by the moonlit river-side
> Groaned the poor Beast—alas! in vain;
> The staff was raised to loftier height,
> And the blows fell with heavier weight
> As Peter struck—and struck again.

Wordsworth is enjoying himself here with a parody of the neo-classical manner. His poet is interrupted by the squire, through whom Wordsworth makes a joke about the advice of Horace—faithfully followed by the poet of 'Peter Bell'—to plunge *in medias res*—into the middle of the story (196–200):

> 'Hold!' cried the Squire, 'against the rules
> Of common sense you're surely sinning;
> This leap is for us all too bold;
> Who Peter was, let that be told
> And start from the beginning.'

This jest is perhaps over-subtle. In the manuscript versions Wordsworth had made it much more obvious, and introduced a punning reference to *Paradise Lost* and *The Divine Comedy*, as well as to Horace.

Wordsworth's simplicity, then, is a deliberate choice of the language of men rather than the conventional language of poetry. It should not be confused with simplicity of mind or of theme. Such poems as 'We are Seven', 'Simon Lee', 'The Thorn', and 'The Idiot Boy'—all published in *Lyrical Ballads* in 1798— have been ridiculed for their crudity, or defended for their homely truth. They remain something of a puzzle, since both those who regard them with contempt and those who defend them seem to be agreed that Wordsworth had no interest in the comic mode, and little sense of humour—an assumption perhaps too lightly made. In 'Peter Bell', written over a period of twenty years, and finally published in 1819, there are many evidences of a lively and even impish sense of humour at work in what has been taken as a 'simple' poem. When a study of the manuscript versions has been made possible by their publication in full, it may be seen that 'Peter Bell' is far from simple or rustic—that it is in fact a witty and intellectually audacious poem. Wordsworth may in these 'simple' poems have failed his readers—or his readers may have failed him—because the poems are too subtle, not because they are too crude. I have omitted any close study of them because I do not share the confidence of some critics that they have been adequately read and thoroughly understood.

That Wordsworth's language is simple only in the sense of not being restricted by a worn-out convention, and that it is as complex as the subject requires, is shown by many poems in *Lyrical Ballads* and elsewhere. 'Tintern Abbey' (1798) uses elevated philosophical language; 'Yew Trees' (1803) uses an elaborate vocabulary and syntax to evoke the dark intricacies of the trees, and the Gothic complexity of the thoughts they suggest:

> Huge trunks! and each particular trunk a growth
> Of intertwisted fibres serpentine
> Up-coiling, and inveterately convolved;

> Nor uninformed with Phantasy, and looks
> That threaten the profane.

In 'Laodamia' (1814) Wordsworth expresses with classical elegance and firmness a Stoic view of human passion. Here Virgil seems to speak again in English verse:

> Yet tears to human suffering are due;
> And mortal hopes defeated and o'erthrown
> Are mourned by man, and not by man alone,
> As fondly he believes.

Wordsworth can also be as elaborately sensuous and exotic as Milton or Spenser, as in the description of the infant's grave in 'The Thorn' (1798) or of the strange splendours of the Americas in 'Ruth' (1799):

> He told of the magnolia, spread
> High as a cloud, high over head!
> The cypress and her spire;
> —Of flowers that with one scarlet gleam
> Cover a thousand leagues, and seem
> To set the hills on fire.

'The Ruined Cottage', written in 1798 and published in Book 1 of *The Excursion* in 1814, appears simple in theme, but its story of a decaying family in a decaying cottage, its garden over-grown with weeds, has deliberate overtones of Milton and the fall of Eve—a theme re-stated by Wordsworth in terms of a hopeless struggle against the blind organic forces of nature: (124–30)

>   Carnations, once
> Prized for surpassing beauty, and no less
> For the peculiar pains they had required,
> Declined their languid heads, wanting support.
> The cumbrous bind-weed, with its wreathes and bells,
> Had twined about her two small rows of peas,
> And dragged them to the earth.

The apparent simplicity is an effect of art; the familiar imagery of the garden is interwoven with recollections of Eve—'herself though fairest unsupported flower', whose flowers,

> Carnation, Purple, Azure, or spect with Gold
> Hung drooping unsustained.

The 'bind-weed, with its wreathes and bells' thus takes on some of the sinister beauty and significance of the serpent with his 'circling spires' in the garden of Eden. The point that has to be made is that Wordsworth is a very conscious and deliberate artist, and—though a rebel against contemporary literary fashions—always conscious of his place in the great tradition of Western poetry.

'The Ruined Cottage' is only one of many poems that amply reward careful reading and re-reading, but for which there has been no room in this study. *The Excursion* itself, though discursive and argumentative rather than poetically inspired, has many backward looks to the myths of the ancient world, and to the visionary life of youth and early manhood. Though this is not a poem to be recommended to the newcomer to Wordsworth, Books I and IV in particular have in them something of the true poetic fire. There are poems of a quiet and sophisticated humour, too long neglected by the critics, notably 'To Joanna' (1798) and 'The Haunted Tree' (1819). The Poems of the Fancy, so classified by Wordsworth, will seem tedious to most modern readers; they are, however, often more interesting than they seem at a first reading, and are usually far from casual. 'The Waggoner' (1805) is an elaborate play of the fancy around the journey of a carter from Kendal to Keswick; it is in effect a calendar poem in the tradition of Ovid's *Fasti*, and associates the disappearance of Waggoner with the onset of winter. 'Hart-Leap Well' (1800) tells the story of a cruel hunt, and proclaims the sanctity of life; the last stanzas have a hauntingly elegiac quality. 'The White Doe of Rylstone' (1807–8) is a historical romance in which Wordsworth seems to be experimenting with

> transmutations
> Rich as the mine's most bright creations.

Without any actual introduction of the supernatural, the white doe is so closely associated with Emily as to suggest that Wordsworth was attempting a metamorphosis, in the manner of Ovid, of maiden into doe, or at least the close identifying of the two. The experiment was not successful, but the poem serves to remind us of Wordsworth's artistic resourcefulness.

The poetry of the later years, with the exception of 'Laodamia', the Duddon sonnets, and a few other poems, is in general considered to be inferior. The 'Ode to Duty' suggests one reason for this—that Wordsworth could not in the long run sustain the burden of imaginative responsibility. The 'Elegiac Stanzas' on Peele Castle, written in 1805, record how the 'deep distress' caused by his brother's loss at sea had 'humanised' the poet's soul. The task of poetic transformation seemed now to be a falsifying of the harsh truths of life:

> Ah! THEN, if mine had been the Painter's hand
> To express what then I saw; and add the gleam,
> The light that never was, on sea or land,
> The consecration, and the Poet's dream;
>
> I would have planted thee, thou hoary Pile
> Amid a world how different from this!
> Beside a sea that should not cease to smile;
> On tranquil land, beneath a sea of bliss.

This is less than fair to his earlier poetry, in which there is little tendency to gloss over the more painful aspects of reality. The shock of his brother's death, however, seems to have strengthened in Wordsworth's mind a distaste for the solitary aloofness of his poetic stance. Life was to be endured rather than enjoyed, and if it was to be endured the solidarity of mankind must be maintained:

> Farewell, farewell, the heart that lives alone,
> Housed in a dream, at distance from the Kind!
> Such happiness, wherever it be known,
> It is to be pitied; for 'tis surely blind.
>
> But welcome fortitude, and patient cheer,
> And frequent sights of what is to be borne!
> Such sights, or worse, as are before me here.
> Not without hope we suffer and we mourn.

The aspiration may well have been to a poetry more closely linked with the common life of man, less the product of solitary contemplation. Wordsworth's best poetry, however, arises from the tension between dream and reality, and when he forsook the dream the reality was left in the light of common day.

The reader of Wordsworth need not be deterred by the problem of his personal beliefs, or his philosophy. It must be remembered that Wordsworth was not a philosopher, but a poet, and that elements of many philosophies, religions, and world systems are to be found in his work, most of them as traditional poetic myth. When such a typically Wordsworthian line occurs as

<blockquote>The silence that is in the starry sky</blockquote>

we might suppose that this is an echo of the 'silence of the infinite spaces' that so much frightened Pascal. This would not mean that Wordsworth shared Pascal's beliefs. Similarly, the echoes of Plato, of the Stoics, the Epicureans, and of Virgil should not lead us to suppose that Wordsworth accepted the systems of belief of ancient philosophers and poets. Like all poets, he made use of beliefs when they could conveniently be shaped into poetic myth; only when this process was no longer possible for him did he settle into a conventional Anglicanism.

The most pervasive myth in Wordsworth is that of the 'one life' within all things. This is so persistent in his early work that his central belief has been identified as pantheism—the making nature itself divine. If to follow the traditional poetic habit of imaginatively giving life to all experience, and of imaginatively unifying all experience, is to be a pantheist, then Wordsworth was a pantheist, in common with the great poets of the classical world. Even the most persistent of poetic habits, however, is not the same as a philosophical or religious belief. When in 'Tintern Abbey', Wordsworth most directly expresses the sense of a unifying spirit within all things, he does so in terms that echo Virgil and Newton; and he immediately questions the validity of this insight as a belief ('If this be but a vain belief'). The identifying of a philosophy in terms of which Wordsworth's poems are to be understood is probably a vain endeavour; but it is also an unnecessary one. Wordsworth's works are each of them individual acts of mind, to be understood poem by poem. Certainly they illuminate each other, and together form a system which itself is

16

all we have of Wordsworth's thought. Too much anxiety about the general pattern may be an obstacle to understanding. The task is to read the poems, and to approach each of them with an alert attention and with the readiness to follow the poet on a mental journey that is often more audacious than it appears to be as one sets out.

2

WORDSWORTH AND THE DAFFODILS

It is all too easy to think of Wordsworth as the simple poet of
simple things. One reason for this is that Wordsworth announced
his intention in the Preface to his *Lyrical Ballads* of 1800, of
using the 'language of men', by which he meant the language of
men who live in the country, and are not given to using learned or
sophisticated language. Wordsworth's subject-matter, moreover, seems often to be simple. He writes of a linnet, a primrose,
a celandine, a lamb, an oak tree, or a robin. The Victorian critics
looked to Wordsworth as a source of the kind of spiritual refreshment and rest they gained from the countryside itself, and
consequently concentrated their attention on those features of
Wordsworth's poetry which appeared to be the simple expressions
of simple thoughts and simple feelings. There are very few
critics who would today take this view of Wordsworth's genius,
but the difficulty remains, not only because of the impression
made by a long tradition of going to Wordsworth for such
memorable simplicities as 'green fields, white sheets of water, and
pure sky', but also by the appearance which Wordsworth's
poems sometimes present of being intellectually relaxed.

The Preface of 1800 to the *Lyrical Ballads* is well known, and
well deserves study. It is a pity that the Advertisement to the
original 1798 edition of *Lyrical Ballads*, included in the 1800
Preface, has not attracted more attention. In his brief introduction to the first edition of his poems, Wordsworth makes claims
for his poetry not easy to reconcile with a view of it as proffering
simple emotions about simple subjects. In the Advertisement,
Wordsworth insists upon two conditions for 'an accurate taste in
poetry'; these are 'severe thought' and 'a long-continued inter-
course with the best models of composition'. Where these two
conditions are not fulfilled, says Wordsworth, 'the judgment may
be erroneous, and...in most cases it necessarily will be so'.

If Wordsworth has been understood as proffering simple emotions, it is largely because this is what readers have looked for in his work. 'I wandered lonely as a cloud' is a useful example. This poem tells the story, which Dorothy Wordsworth also records in her *Journal*, of Wordsworth's coming upon daffodils while walking in the Lake District. At a first reading it seems to be merely an anecdote, a part of the poet's life-history that he has put into verse. Yet it has, as we know, a strangely haunting power. The mere vitality of the rhythms and the liveliness of the language could scarcely account for so permanent an appeal; without some intellectual life it is unlikely that the poem could remain interesting for so long.

Wordsworth himself considered this poem to be one of the touchstones of a reader's capacity to understand his work, and at the same time made it clear that he did not himself think it at all trivial. In a letter to Francis Wragham he says:

You mentioned the Daffodils; you know Butler...; when I was in Town in Spring he happened to see the volumes lying on Montague's mantelpiece and to glance his eye upon this very Poem of the Daffodils; 'Aye', says he, 'a fine morsel this for the Reviewers.' When this was told me, for I was not present, I observed that there were two lines in that little poem which if thoroughly felt would annihilate nine tenths of the Reviews of the Kingdom, as they would find no Readers; the lines I alluded to, were those

'They flash upon that inward eye,
Which is the bliss of solitude.'

(*Letters of William and Dorothy Wordsworth*, ed. E. de Selincourt, Oxford University Press, 1935–9, *The Middle Years*, vol. I, p. 149.)

Wordsworth, moreover, says of this poem, and of another which he describes as 'the Rock crowned with snowdrops', that 'whoever is much pleased with either of these quiet and tender delineations must be fitted to walk through the recesses of my poetry with delight, and will there recognize, at every turn, something or other in which, and over which, it has that property and right which knowledge and love confer'. We thus have Wordsworth's own word for it that 'I wandered lonely' was intended to provide not only delight, but also 'that property and right which knowledge and love confer'. The reader may well ask himself what 'knowledge' is offered by poems of this kind.

'I wandered lonely as a cloud' is only superficially about the daffodils which Wordsworth remembers so vividly. What it offers us in fact is an account of the experience of poetic creation. The poem opens with the poet wandering in a state of loneliness and passivity. When he says that he 'wandered lonely as a cloud' he reminds us of those moods when we are aimless, undirected, and not fully related to the world around us. This sense of disconnectedness from experience is strengthened by the description of the clouds which 'float on high'. The mood of detachment, or rather of indifference and passivity, is suddenly broken in upon by the appearance of the daffodils:

> When all at once I saw a crowd,
> A host, of golden daffodils.

These very lines show the poetic process itself at work. At first the daffodils are seen as 'a crowd'; but with a sudden shift of attention and a sudden energy of mind the poet slightly re-arranges the pattern they form in his mind, and sees them as 'a host'. In other words the shapelessness, as of a crowd, which the daffodils at first seemed to exhibit, is turned into a pattern, though not a rigid one—the order of an army like the host of angels in *Paradise Lost* rather than the drill order of the barrack-square. The poet's mind is already at work ordering the experience that flows into it, giving it coherence and vividness. The vividness appears immediately in the heightening of the colour of the daffodils from yellow to 'golden'. This process, by which the objects seen in the landscape are invested with brightness and coherence by the poet's own mind, is described in the rest of the poem. What we are learning of, then, is not Wordsworth's chance meeting with a number of yellow wild-flowers, but the experience of a poet who has imposed upon the disorderly facts of the world an order and a brightness which his own imagination brings to them. What we are offered is not only a result of the poetic process, but also an account of it.

Wordsworth spends no words on a detailed description of the daffodils. Instead, he describes them as:

> Beside the lake, beneath the trees,
> Fluttering and dancing in the breeze.

The daffodils are placed in relationship to the lake and the trees. Daffodils grow best in the shade and where there is water, and so the flowers are not accidentally at this particular point in space and time. The curve they describe along the lake is the curve of necessity, and it is immediately related by Wordsworth's active intelligence to the very curve of the heavens:

> Continuous as the stars that shine
> And twinkle on the milky way,
> They stretched in never-ending line
> Along the margin of a bay:
> Ten thousand saw I at a glance,
> Tossing their heads in sprightly dance.

In these lines Wordsworth shows the daffodils as part of a universal order, as growing where they do because of the natural law which dictates their existence. Just as the stars in the Milky Way are fixed in their courses, and show a beauty which arises from necessity, so the daffodils are triumphantly themselves in their own particular place and time. There is a poignancy here because in all creation man seems to be the only creature that is capable of feeling not at home, of 'wandering lonely as a cloud'; and, unlike the cloud, being aware of his loneliness and his lack of a settled habitation. The joy exhibited by both the 'dancing' flowers and the stars that 'twinkle' is attributed to them by the poet, as he well understands. This joy is the counterpart of the loneliness and passivity experienced by the poet until his mind was awakened to new life by the daffodils themselves. Even while this thought is being advanced, the poet's mind is actively imposing a further pattern upon the daffodils. They are described as 'fluttering and dancing in the breeze'; so there is a leap of the mind from seeing the movements of the daffodils as a mere disorganized 'fluttering' to a perception that it is a kind of dance, a harmonious movement in which a pattern may be discerned. In this the flowers resemble the stars, in whose movements men from Newton's time onwards—and Wordsworth was educated in Cambridge to a deep respect for Newton—had increasingly learned to discover a comprehensible and even delightful pattern.

The daffodils are not only linked with the stars and the heavens; they are also compared with the waves on the lake, which also dance, though not it seems with so much 'glee' as the flowers. (The word 'glee' is a curious one, which Wordsworth most commonly uses when talking of the joy of creative activity.) The waves are acted upon by the force of the wind, and, as water is a fairly simple substance, the pattern of response is comparatively limited. The daffodils, however, being more complex and organic forms of life, 'dance' with more resilience and with more complex patterns under the pressure of the breeze. For this reason Wordsworth finds the patterns more intricate, and more delightful, and finds a more joyful life in the flowers than in the waves. This is an important feature of the poem. Writing to Sir George Beaumont, Wordsworth complains of a friend of Sir George's, who has remarked on Wordsworth's poem and described it as being 'on daffodils reflected in the water'. Wordsworth is outraged by this comment, and writes:

What shall we think of criticism or judgment founded upon, and exemplified by a Poem which must have been so inattentively perused? My language is precise; and therefore it would be false modesty to charge myself with blame;

> . . . 'beneath the trees,
> *Fluttering and dancing* in the breeze.
>
> The waves *beside* them danced; but they
> Out-did the *sparkling waves* in glee.'

Can expression be more distinct? And let me ask your friend how it is possible for flowers to be reflected in the water where there are *waves*? They may indeed in *still* water, but the whole object of my poem is the trouble or agitation, both of the flowers and the water. I must needs respect the understanding of every one honoured by your friendship, but sincerity compels me to say that my poems must be more nearly looked at before they can give rise to any remarks of much value, even from the strongest minds.

(*Letters, The Middle Years*, vol. I, p. 170)

This comment is a further sign that Wordsworth took this poem seriously, and expected his readers to take it seriously too. He is horrified by a reader who is so careless and inattentive, and so ignorant of the natural world, that he fails to see that the daffodils cannot possibly be reflected in the water while they are dancing in a breeze. The breeze is important to Wordsworth, not only as an essential element in the poem in which rhythmic patterns of water, and the rhythmic dance of the flowers, form so large a part of the pleasure, but also because, for Wordsworth, a breeze or wind is a common symbol of the creative activity of the poet. The breeze that blows on the lake and sets the waves and daffodils dancing is the natural equivalent of the breeze of poetic 'glee' which is now blowing through the poet's mind. So Wordsworth declares:

> The waves beside them danced; but they
> Out-did the sparkling waves in glee:
> A poet could not but be gay,
> In such a jocund company:

provides delight

The poet is gay because his mind is once more active, making order in a world which seemed so short a time ago disorderly and pointless. Where he was lonely, he is now in 'a jocund company'. It should be noted, however, that Wordsworth does not say that nobody could fail to be gay in such a situation. He speaks here of 'a poet'. The poet, although he is essentially like other men—'a man speaking to men'—has, according to Wordsworth, a 'greater organic sensibility', and has usually 'thought long and deeply'. It is such a man, and such a man only, who finds himself in a state of creative joy when placed in such a situation.

in the mind of poet

The poet, moreover, is not limited to the immediate pleasure of intellectual delight in the scene observed:

> I gazed—and gazed—but little thought
> What wealth the show to me had brought:
>
> For oft, when on my couch I lie
> In vacant or in pensive mood,
> They flash upon that inward eye
> Which is the bliss of solitude;

> And then my heart with pleasure fills,
> And dances with the daffodils.

What is described here is the poet's power, not only of organizing experience so that it is coherent and delightful, but also of re-calling that experience at future times. Though Wordsworth does not say so, this is evidently because the creative artist organizes the experience in a formal pattern of words, or if he is a musician in a formal pattern of notes, or if a painter, in a pattern of pig-ments. Consequently the experience is not lost, but may be recovered when it is wanted. So the delight in creative perception recurs when the poet finds himself in need of it—when he is once more 'in vacant or in pensive mood', as he was in his loneliness at the beginning of the poem. When the poetic process makes the experience available once again the daffodils 'flash upon that inward eye Which is the bliss of solitude'. Where the poet was lonely at the beginning of the poem he now talks of 'the bliss of solitude'; this kind of solitude is very different from the melan-choly loneliness which is described at the beginning of the poem. In this condition the poet finds his heart dancing with joy, a joy which revives the pleasure participated in when the poet observed the dance of the daffodils in the breeze.

In 'Peter Bell' Wordsworth says of the unregenerate Peter, who brings only a 'hardness' of eye to the natural world, that

> A primrose by a river's brim,
> A yellow primrose was to him,
> And it was nothing more.

When the poet's eye falls upon the flowers, they become, not merely what they would have been to Peter—a row of yellow daffodils, but 'a host of *golden* daffodils'. The suggestion of a treasure created by the poetic imagination, and not merely dis-covered by chance, is continued when the poet's eye dwells on the 'show':

> I gazed—and gazed—but little thought
> What wealth the show to me had brought.

The rhythms fall with a special insistent emphasis on the *gazing*, an act of mind in which the poetic transformation takes place spontaneously, without full consciousness on the poet's part of what he is doing, just as a master chess-player makes his moves as if by unconscious thought. The emphasis on 'to me' in the next line might seem strange, if it were not that Wordsworth is here describing what happens to a poet, and to himself as a poet. The 'wealth' which is available for future years is created by the poet's touch of gold, which transforms into brightness and radiance the most commonplace and trivial of details. To read these lines, as some have done, as suggesting a mindless or merely passive staring, is radically to misunderstand them. When Wordsworth *gazes*, he is performing an act of intellectual concentration so complete that it leaves no room for self-consciousness. It is only afterwards, in recollection, that the act is understood and described. This poem provides a useful illustration of Wordsworth's view of poetry as the 'spontaneous overflow of powerful feelings'. When quoted out of its context, this remark seems to support the view of Wordsworth as an 'emotional' poet; but the rest of the sentence insists that poems of any value can rarely be written except by men of 'more than usual organic sensibility' who have 'thought long and deeply'. The 'spontaneous overflow of powerful feelings' is more akin to the joy with which Archimedes cried 'Eureka!' after solving his problem, or to the delight felt in any intellectual discovery, than to the expression of simple human sentiments of love, anger, fear, or hope. When the poet saw the daffodils, he 'little thought' what they meant to him. The thought came later, and the poem is the record of that thought, and of the intellectual delight it offers.

Wordsworth in this poem is describing an experience of which all are capable, but which is increasingly neglected as men become preoccupied with businesses and professions. It is the imagination that enables man to enter into and give life and significance to the world. This is essentially an intellectual process, by which the mind and powers of feeling are brought to the contemplation of what lies before the eyes. The world has significance, life, and joy in proportion to the intelligence, energy, and pleasure we ourselves bring to it. Wordsworth in this poem describes as a poet how, on one particular occasion, the poetic process worked for him, and how he found it recurring at later times. Even this apparently simple poem, then, is not so much the story of a nature poet remembering some pretty flowers, as an intelligent and subtle account of the creative process itself.

In 'The Reverie of Poor Susan', which he composed in 1797 and published in 1800, Wordsworth describes the effect upon a country girl who is living in the city of the song of a thrush heard at a street corner. This poem was deliberately placed by Wordsworth next to 'I wandered lonely as a cloud', with the comment that it showed the same capacity of the mind to respond to 'a simple impression'. The difference here is that 'poor Susan' is not a poet, and she is therefore at the mercy of the laws of association, which call up memories which she is unable to organize or control, and which she cannot recall at will. When the thrush sings, Susan remembers her home in the country, and sees a mountain, 'a vision of trees' and a river flowing through the city of London. She remembers also her childhood in the country and the happiness of the home that she loves. But unlike the poet of 'I wandered lonely as a cloud' she remains passive, and can only remain helpless as the vision vanishes for ever:

> She looks, and her heart is in heaven: but they fade,
> The mist and the river, the hill and the shade:
> The stream will not flow, and the hill will not rise,
> And the colours have all passed away from her eyes!

The distinction between these two experiences was for Wordsworth an important one. He had in his early days fallen under the influence of the theory of memory and of knowledge propounded by Hartley, who held that the operation of the mind was essentially mechanical and automatic. If this was true, there was no room for the creative activity of the poetic imagination. 'I wandered lonely as a cloud' not only describes this act of creative power; it also asserts its validity. The contrast between the poet who can give permanent life to his experience, and the 'poor Susans' of this world, who depend upon the fitful coming and going of the fancy as the laws of memory dictate, is illustrated by these two poems which Wordsworth placed side by side, and linked together with his note on the workings of the imagination.

26

It must not be thought that Wordsworth sets poets and ordinary men and women apart; on the contrary, the poet is 'a man speaking to men', and all men have within them the capacity for poetry, or at least for the brightness and unity of perception which may be called the poetic vision. He insists in *The Prelude* that the 'poetic spirit' exists in all men from childhood, though in most men it is overlaid by habit:

> Such, verily, is the first
> Poetic spirit of our human life,
> By uniform control of after years,
> In most, abated or suppressed; in some
> Pre-eminent till death.
>
> (II, 260–4)

'Poor Susan', who lives in the city, can catch only a passing glimpse of the radiance of her childhood. She is one of those in whom the 'poetic spirit' has been 'abated or suppressed'. Wordsworth, however, insists that all men may recover the use of the poetic faculty within them, however much it has been overlaid by habit:

> 'tis thine,
> The prime and vital principle is thine
> In the recesses of thy nature...
>
> (*The Prelude*, XIV, 214–16)

When Wordsworth writes of the poetic spirit, he writes of what he believes is important to all men. The poet is 'a man speaking to men' above all when he writes of the poetic spirit, for when he does this he speaks to what is most valuable to all men—the vital principle of perception with which they shape their own reality. Wordsworth's many poems on the poet and his task are not the products of an ivory tower, but of a mind deeply concerned to speak to other minds and awaken them to their own capacity for delight. His choice of simple words and his treatment of simple natural objects in so many of his earlier poems is in no sense naïve; it testifies to a determination to speak as directly as possible to the minds of men, and not merely to the literary public. The poet's task was to contribute to 'joy in widest commonalty spread'.

This interest in the creative powers of the human mind, which we have already seen in 'I wandered lonely' and 'The Reverie of Poor Susan', is the central preoccupation in the poems of the early period.

'To the Cuckoo' (1802), for example, deals with the 'two-fold shout' of the cuckoo, which appears in the poem as an echo of the poet's childhood. Wordsworth is not much interested in the cuckoo for itself, but only as an image of recurrent experience, and as a reminder of the spring-time of his own life:

> Thrice welcome, darling of the Spring!
> Even yet thou art to me
> No bird, but an invisible thing,
> A voice, a mystery.

The cuckoo's song is the voice of the poet's own boyhood; it is a link with a time of youthful eagerness and hope:

> The same whom in my schoolboy days
> I listened to, that Cry
> Which made me look a thousand ways
> In bush, and tree, and sky.

The song is in itself a mere 'babbling'; but for the poet it is a link with his former condition, a reminder of the visionary hours of childhood, and a promise of the recovery of the paradisal state:

> Though babbling only to the Vale
> Of sunshine and of flowers,
> Thou bringest unto me a tale
> Of visionary hours.

The cuckoo in this poem, like the owls in 'There was a Boy', is the associative link in a process by which the poet's imagination is roused to give life and significance to the world around him. In his schooldays the cuckoo's 'Cry'—in common of course with many other such experiences—kindled his eager interest in the world about him:

> To seek thee did I often rove
> Through woods and on the green;
> And thou wert still a hope, a love;
> Still longed for, never seen.

When the song is heard again in later years it recalls the joy of youth, by its associative power flooding the mind with the recollection:

> And I can listen to thee yet;
> Can lie upon the plain
> And listen, till I do beget
> That golden time again.

This stanza gives an account of the poetic process itself. The poet listens to the song of the cuckoo, the repetition of 'listen' suggesting a careful and sustained attention. The result of this attention to the voice that recalls his past experience is that the poet is enabled to 'beget' the 'golden time'. As elsewhere, Wordsworth here suggests that the poet's task is to recover the unity of the world of experience as it was known in childhood, and so to 'beget' the paradisal condition. In this task he is aided by those experiences of daily life which connect his later life with his childhood, so that his days are

> Bound each to each by natural piety.

The task also calls for meditation; he listens to the voice of the cuckoo with the same intensity with which he 'gazed and gazed' on the daffodils. It is not the cuckoo that begets the golden time, but the poet; it is he who through the power of imagination creates a world of delight. The bird is 'blessed' only because it has provided the occasion for this poetic transformation:

> O blessed Bird! the earth we pace
> Again appears to be
> An unsubstantial, faery place;
> That is fit home for Thee!

This is not in any serious sense a poem about a cuckoo. The cuckoo is of little more importance to Wordsworth's thought than is the crumb of cake to Proust's account of the recovery of past time. All that matters is that it is an elusive bird with an echoing song. This information is provided by Wordsworth in the poem, so that it can be read perfectly well even by those many readers of English who have never heard a cuckoo in their lives.

This method, applied to a wider range of natural objects,

may be seen at work in 'There was a Boy', first published as a complete poem in the 1800 edition of *Lyrical Ballads*. Words-worth later included this poem in *The Prelude*, and for this reason it is sometimes thought of as a personal account of an experience in his boyhood, and the features of the poem which tend to make it less personal and more universal are perhaps given too little attention. In this poem, as it stands, the boy is not the poet—he is simply 'a Boy'. What Wordsworth has to say is of course drawn from his own boyhood experience, but the poem is more than an account of a private event. It is a statement about the status of a living human being in a universe of natural law, which gives back to his voice only its own mocking echo, and which allows itself to be disturbed only slightly by his shouts, settling quietly back into its accustomed pattern when his voice falls silent.

The poem begins with a quiet statement of the transitoriness of the experience recorded, and even of the boy's existence:

> There was a Boy; ye knew him well, ye cliffs
> And islands of Winander!

The poet addresses not the boy—who is now dead—but the cliffs and islands that have outlasted him. From the cliffs and lakes of the immediate foreground the scene is widened to take in the whole order of the natural world within which the boy has lived:

> —many a time,
> At evening, when the earliest stars began
> To move along the edges of the hills,
> Rising or setting, would he stand alone,
> Beneath the trees, or by the glimmering lake.

The regular movement of the stars, rising in the east or setting in the west, suggests the daily turning of the earth, and the movement of time itself. It is in this context of the vast spaces of the universe and the inexorable movement of time that the boy is placed 'Beneath the trees, or by the glimmering lake'. The trees, in contrast with the stars, are subject to change and decay; the word 'glimmering' suggests a temporary appearance rather than a steady state. The boy himself is in this way given a temporary and uncertain position in the natural order. As if to challenge the imperturbable order that confronts him the boy imitates the hooting of the owls in calls that resound and echo over the lake:

> And there, with fingers interwoven, both hands
> Pressed closely palm to palm and to his mouth
> Uplifted, he, as through an instrument,
> Blew mimic hootings to the silent owls,
> That they might answer him.—And they would shout
> Across the watery vale, and shout again,
> Responsive to his call,—with quivering peals,
> And long halloos, and screams, and echoes loud
> Redoubled and redoubled; concourse wild
> Of jocund din.

The boy succeeds in arousing an echo, wild and joyful, from the otherwise silent world before him. The activity—as the use of this passage in *The Prelude* suggests—is that of a boy who is akin to the poet. He blows though his hands as through an 'instrument', and calls up a responsive though disturbing voice from the world around him. This voice, like the poet's, is, however, in one sense merely a redoubled echo of his own. The sense that the world is at once all too solid and immovable, and yet strangely unreal, that 'mirror on mirror mirrored is all the show', is subtly conveyed by these lines.

The uproar is followed by an intensified silence:

> And, when there came a pause
> Of silence such as baffled his best skill:
> Then sometimes, in that silence, while he hung
> Listening, a gentle shock of mild surprise
> Has carried far into his heart the voice
> Of mountain-torrents; or the visible scene
> Would enter unawares into his mind,
> With all its solemn imagery, its rocks,
> Its woods, and that uncertain heaven received
> Into the bosom of the steady lake.

In the silence that follows, there is a moment of quiet in which the very voice of the natural scene is heard. Behind the noise made by the boy and the owls there is a quieter and more persistent sound, the 'voice of mountain-torrents'. This more abiding voice is that of the ultimate physical forces that persist through the more temporary noises that disturb the peace of the scene. The boy is said to have

                                        hung
            Listening...

What is suggested by the word 'hung' is a moment of suspension of time in which the boy discovers with 'a shock of mild surprise' what lies beneath the confused appearances of things. The world he inhabits is a world of echoes and mirror-images, behind which the more permanent physical forces steadily assert themselves. The echoes he has awakened die away, and the ripples on the lake subside, restoring the steady reflection. The passage conveys the notion of a nature ruled by absolute laws of which the echoes and images of our own experience are merely fleeting expressions. They die away, leaving only the distant sound of the mountain-torrents and the smooth surface of the 'steady lake'.

The death of the boy is not, as some critics have suggested, a merely sentimental–romantic conclusion. On the contrary, it is the necessary completion of the poem. The boy's life is almost as temporary as the echoes and images of the lake. His death is a re-enactment of the silence that fell on him when he 'hung Listening'—the parallel is established by a repetition of the word:

                            the churchyard *hangs*
            Upon a slope above the village-school.

The ultimate silence broods over all human lives; the 'village-school' serves here to make the boy more widely representative. The poem ends on a note of intense meditation rather than deep feeling:

            On summer-evenings, I believe that there
            A long half-hour together I have stood
            Mute—looking at the grave in which he lies!

The pattern established by the boy who 'hung' in silence over the lake, and the churchyard that 'hangs' over the village-school, is repeated here, with the poet standing 'mute'—silenced by thought —over the grave. The poem expresses with great force and clarity

4

THE 'MATTHEW' POEMS

The three 'Matthew' poems, written in 1799 and placed by Wordsworth together in *Poems of Sentiment and Reflection*, are well worth attention for their own sakes. They will serve to show how, for Wordsworth, the life of man and the task of the poet are interdependent. They also provide an illustration of the use made by Wordsworth of natural objects as part of a poetic language of his own devising—a language with which he achieves an unusual compression and strength. The three poems are similar in form; the first, openly elegiac in manner, uses lines of four feet throughout, and is somewhat less dramatic than the other two. In these the traditional ballad metre is used, a form that is well suited to dramatic inversions and ironies. The short line of three feet that is used alternately with the four-foot line provides the intermittent emphasis that is needed for a more dramatic style. The three poems are linked together by a common theme and a common style, and by Wordsworth's own placing of them together in his collected works. They also show a progression of thought, from contemplation of an individual life to a more general consideration of man's condition. The language, as is to be expected in ballads, is simple and sometimes bald, but this ought not to lead the reader to suppose that these are simple poems. They are works of considerable subtlety and sophistication, both in poetic detail and in structure.

The first of the poems—simply entitled 'Matthew'—is a meditation on the gilt letters of Matthew's name on a tablet giving the names of former schoolmasters. Wordsworth later said that these poems 'would not gain by a literal detail of facts', that he was not thinking only of schoolmasters, and that 'this Schoolmaster was made up of several both of his class and of other occupations'. It seems certain that the original impulse that gave rise to the 'Matthew' poems was gratitude to William Taylor, the headmaster of Hawkshead School, who died when Wordsworth was a schoolboy there. This was thirteen years before the composition of the 'Matthew' poems, in which Matthew, as Wordsworth indicates, has ceased to be any particular person; even his occupation as a schoolmaster is no longer important. What is important is that Matthew is a man who lives to the full, experiencing the world with an unusual capacity for joy and an unusually lively consciousness:

> The sighs which Matthew heaved were sighs
> Of one tired out with fun and madness;
> The tears which came to Matthew's eyes
> Were tears of light, the dew of gladness.

This vital energy goes with a capacity for deep thought and feeling:

> Yet sometimes, when the secret cup
> Of still and serious thought went round,
> It seemed as if he drank it up—
> He felt with spirit so profound.

Matthew may be understood as Wordsworth's idea of a good man; he is a source of love and joy because he is himself joyful. He has a gift of spontaneous 'fun and madness', as well as a capacity for deep thought, thought that is *felt*, not merely a mental game. This idea of the good man is also, it must be noted, Wordsworth's idea of the poet. He too is 'a man of more than usual organic sensibility', and he too must be capable of thinking 'long and deeply'. The poet, for Wordsworth, is a representative man; and a man is happy and good inasmuch as he shares the poet's capacity for delight and for lively consciousness. The 'Matthew' poems provide us at one and the same time with a meditation on the life of a good man and a meditation on the task of the poet.

'Matthew' is concerned with the life of such a man, and with the mystery of his death. Those who have in them something of Matthew's qualities will, the narrator says, be able to respond to the poem:

> If Nature, for a favourite child,
> In thee hath tempered so her clay,

That every hour thy heart runs wild,
Yet never once doth go astray,

Read o'er these lines...

Vital spontaneity without confusion or loss of control is the end to which Nature has successfully 'tempered so her clay'—the suggestion is of a human life mysteriously moulded from physical elements, and then dissolved, as it seems, into nothingness once again:

> Poor Matthew, all his frolics o'er
> Is silent as a standing pool;
> Far from the chimney's merry roar,
> And murmur of the village school.

The two principles of Matthew's life are represented here by 'the chimney's merry roar'—the vital warmth expressed in a homely metaphor—and the 'murmur of the village school', which evokes in a humble way the task of intellect in the kindling of the mind. The 'frolics' which are now over remind the reader that Matthew retained through life a childlike quality; his final silence has fallen on him as sleep falls on a child. There remains the question of survival. Is there anything left of Matthew?

> —Thou soul of God's best earthly mould!
> Thou happy Soul! and can it be
> That these two words of glittering gold
> Are all that must remain of thee?

The soul is from an 'earthly mould', and the answer to the question seems to be that it is dissolved with the dissolution of the body. What remains of Matthew is that he has become for Wordsworth a model or poetic idea of the 'happy Soul'.

The union of a vital power of joy with full consciousness is a condition of Matthew's 'goodness'. It is also a union for which there is a price to pay, for to be fully conscious and fully alive is to be exposed to pain. This is the irony that Wordsworth explores in the next of the three poems—'The Two April Mornings'.

The poem begins with the promise of hope and joy given by a

spring morning, as the narrator and Matthew set out on a holiday walk:

> We walked along, while bright and red
> Uprose the morning sun.

For no apparent reason, Matthew is plunged into an inner meditation:

> And Matthew stopped, he looked, and said,
> 'The will of God be done!'

To all outward appearance, Matthew has every reason to be happy:

> A village schoolmaster was he,
> With hair of glittering grey;
> As blithe a man as you could see
> On a spring holiday.
>
> And on that morning, through the grass,
> And by the steaming rills,
> We travelled merrily, to pass
> A day among the hills.

The word 'glittering', used of grey hair, echoes the 'glittering gold' of the previous poem, and suggests that Matthew wears his grey hairs like a golden crown won from experience; it does not at first occur to the narrator that the rising sun, the radiant morning, and the warmth that causes the mists to rise from the brooks can be anything but occasions for joy. He questions Matthew about his sudden change of mood:

> 'Our work,' said I, 'was well begun,
> Then from thy breast what thought,
> Beneath so beautiful a sun,
> So sad a sigh has brought?'

It is notable that the narrator refers to the holiday as their 'work'; the joyful excursion into the hills is represented as a task they have undertaken in common, as it is a poet's task to explore the country of joy. The question raised is directed to Matthew, but it is a question asked of human life in general: how can we be unhappy when there is so much cause for joy, and no immediate cause for sorrow?

Matthew stops once more, and gives a surprisingly elaborate answer. What it amounts to is a demonstration that man cannot live only in the immediate present, that he is the sum of all that he has experienced, and that at any moment a chance perception may call up levels of experience that seemed to be deeply buried and even lost. The April morning, for all its display of freshness and new life, cannot give a new life to Matthew; it can only call to the surface the memory of Aprils gone by, and of the life that then was new.

> 'Yon cloud with that long purple cleft
> Brings fresh into my mind
> A day like this which I have left
> Full thirty years behind.
>
> 'And just above yon slope of corn
> Such colours, and no other,
> Were in the sky, that April morn,
> Of this the very brother.'

Matthew for all his blitheness is at the mercy of time, which not only takes away what he loves, but also presents him with inescapable reminders—a cloud, a colour, a quality of light—of what has been lost and of what might have been.

> 'With rod and line I sued the sport
> Which that sweet season gave,
> And, to the churchyard come, stopped short
> Beside my daughter's grave.'

With unobtrusive art, Wordsworth has made Matthew 'stop' twice in the story; when he is now remembering how he 'stopped short' at the grave it comes with an accumulated dramatic force. This is, however, only the beginning of what Matthew is reminded of by the April morning.

The next stanzas provide a recollection of what the daughter was, and a thought of what she might have been:

> 'Nine summers had she scarcely seen,
> The pride of all the vale;
> And then she sang;—she would have been
> A very nightingale.'

49

The little girl's singing was not yet that of a nightingale—that she 'would have been A very nightingale' implies that if she had lived she would have attained a power of love and joy such as is expressed traditionally by the song of the nightingale. This attestation of loss and waste is followed by what seems an almost brutally direct statement of the fact of death:

> 'Six feet in earth my Emma lay;
> And yet I loved her more,
> For so it seemed, than till that day
> I e'er had loved before.'

The mere fact that Emma is dead, flatly stated as it is, is only the beginning of the anguish described. This arises from the irony by which Matthew's deepest love for Emma can only be realized through her loss. If this is true of all human love, it is clear that life can never offer a surplus of joy, but only of pain. The quiet phrasing should not disguise the tragic and ironic implications.

Matthew has been reminded of his Emma by seeing a cloud which reminds him of a day when he happened to see his daughter's grave. On that occasion, too, as he remembers, a further reminder was given him by a girl who happened to pass by and whose appearance twisted the knife in the wound:

> 'And, turning from her grave, I met,
> Beside the churchyard yew,
> A blooming Girl, whose hair was wet
> With points of morning dew.'

The poetic links between the girl remembered and the April morning are provided by the suggestion of spring in 'blooming' and by the 'points of morning dew' in her hair. She has almost the appearance of Flora, or of a nymph of spring; the basket on her head evokes the figures in a classic frieze:

> 'A basket on her head she bare;
> Her brow was smooth and white:
> To see a child so very fair,
> It was a pure delight!'

Here the suggestions are of a golden age of innocence and joy. The girl's brow is 'smooth and white', she is 'so very fair', and she gives to the gazer not merely 'delight', but 'a pure delight'. She has, moreover, an elemental vitality:

> 'No fountain from its rocky cave
> E'er tripped with foot so free;
> She seemed as happy as a wave
> That dances on the sea.'

The girl passing by, thirty years before, is in this way given a visionary quality; she appears like a revenant, presenting to the imagination what Matthew's Emma might have been, and did not become. The very joy that the sight of the girl offers is an even profounder source of pain.

> 'There came from me a sigh of pain
> Which I could ill confine;
> I looked at her, and looked again:
> And did not wish her mine!'

This is quietly said, but it contains an adverse verdict on life· The price that is paid by consciousness and by love is one that would not be willingly offered if it could be foreseen. The spring-goddess offers a 'pure delight' which man's condition inevitably turns to pain. Matthew's Emma is a memory within a memory within his mind, yet she still appears to trouble the morning scene, like a ghost that cannot be appeased.

The story itself is now placed by the poet in the past:

> Matthew is in his grave, yet now,
> Methinks, I see him stand,
> As at that moment, with a bough
> Of wilding in his hand.

The 'bough of wilding' is a branch from a sapling, a fruit tree that has seeded itself outside the orchard, and has grown wild in the hedgerow or the forest, giving only bitter fruit. In the poet's memory Matthew lives on, fixed in the immobility of pain; yet this is 'As blithe a man as you could see'. The whole poem suggests that man is doomed to defeat by his very nature, that his very capacity for joy exposes him to pain, and that his power of imagining the good leaves him with an endless and growing sense of loss. The final lines of 'The Two April Mornings', in which Matthew, now in his grave, is remembered as standing with 'a bough of wilding' in his hand, is one that lingers in the mind. The 'bough of wilding' is perhaps a gentle reminder of the bough carried by Aeneas in the Underworld on his visit to the dead. Matthew has gone deep into his own underworld, and returned alone.

The last of the three poems, 'The Fountain', appears at a first reading to be fairly simple and almost artless, yet when it is looked at more closely it also reveals a great complexity of art. The opening lines are straightforward:

> We talked with open heart, and tongue
> Affectionate and true,
> A pair of friends, though I was young,
> And Matthew seventy-two.

The poem brings together a young man and an old man, not as strangers, but as friends; the reason for this, as we see later, is that the poem is to attempt an honest account of man's relationship to time and to the world, and to express such truths as can be exchanged only by friends. One of the themes of the poem is the ultimate separateness of human beings, and this is prepared for in these lines. There is nothing between the poet and Matthew but a difference of age; they are friends, and speak with open hearts to each other. But the open hearts and the 'tongue Affectionate and true' are, as we see later, not enough to remove their final solitariness. The difference in age serves to introduce the theme of time, and of man's subjection to it; we see 'a man young and old' in the two figures of the poet and Matthew.

> We lay beneath a spreading oak,
> Beside a mossy seat;
> And from the turf a fountain broke,
> And gurgled at our feet.

The young man and the old man placed together suggest the theme of time; the oak tree beneath which they lie is an image of duration, the 'fountain' or spring that rises at their feet is made in the poem into an image of emerging life. The word 'gurgle' is of course an echo of the sound of the spring, but it has associations with the gurgling of an infant; these are strictly subordinate to the literal sense, but they colour the phrase with a suggestion of birth and childhood. The 'mossy seat' is a more subtle reminder of mortality; the associations of moss with chill and gloom are enough to cast a shadow over the scene. So as the old man and the young man lie talking side by side they are placed in the context of birth, duration, and death. All this is done with a quiet art that may be missed by a casual reader, or even mistaken for artlessness.

> 'Now, Matthew!' said I, 'let us match
> This water's pleasant tune
> With some old border-song, or catch
> That suits a summer's noon;
>
> 'Or of the church-clock and the chimes
> Sing here beneath the shade,
> That half-mad thing of witty rhymes
> Which you last April made!'

The young man finds the sound of the running water pleasing to his ear; he is complacently happy, and asks Matthew to join with him in a ballad, a catch, or in the witty rhymes made 'last April' by the old man. These were 'about the crazy old church-clock' and represented a momentary defiance of time, a defiance which was 'half-mad', and was made 'last April'—a season of hope and of folly. The young man wishes to recapture this joyous defiance of the clock and of time. Such a song suits 'a summer's noon', and the noontide of life. The young man can happily enjoy 'witty rhymes' about time; the old man is not so sure that poetry and song can any longer reassure him.

Matthew's answer is that of a man who has at last been defeated; there is a strong irony, brought out by the contrast with 'grey-haired', in the use of the word 'glee'; because his 'glee' belongs to an earlier Matthew, who has now been almost overborne by age and weakness:

> In silence Matthew lay, and eyed
> The spring beneath the tree;
> And thus the dear old Man replied,
> The grey-haired man of glee.

Matthew is 'a man of glee'; he is a singer of border-songs and catches, and a maker of 'witty rhymes'. Here, as elsewhere in Wordsworth, the word 'glee' is used to refer to creative delight. The 'grey-haired man of glee' is a poet in his old age—the placing of the young poet and his older counterpart together creates a dialogue between the poet young and the poet old.

Matthew looks at 'the spring beneath the tree' in a brooding silence, in which he contemplates his own journey from birth to the brink of death. The expression 'dear old Man' has a double sense; it is a conventional phrase, and capable of bearing the weight of feeling which will emerge when the young man has understood what is in Matthew's mind. The old man's reply comes after a lengthy pause:

> 'No check, no stay, this Streamlet fears;
> How merrily it goes!
> 'Twill murmur on a thousand years,
> And flow as now it flows.'

The bitter reflection prompted by the stream is that human life, though like Matthew's it may go on 'merrily' enough for a time, will certainly not do so for 'a thousand years', like the stream. This brings him to the source of his pain—that the unchanging fountain is the very one by which he has often lain when 'a vigorous man':

> 'And here, on this delightful day,
> I cannot choose but think
> How oft, a vigorous man, I lay
> Beside this fountain's brink.'

Matthew's tone is conversational and level, but its very quietness intensifies the painfulness of what he is contemplating. The 'delightful day' is partly a casual remark about the weather, partly an ironic comment on the delight felt by the younger man and the desolate state of the older. The quietness and slowness of the phrasing gives the old man a patriarchal dignity of speech, so that he seems to speak for more than himself. It is not for nothing that Wordsworth calls him 'the old Man'—even the capital letter adds something to his representative character. The idiomatic and

54

conversational phrase 'I cannot choose but think', with its double
negative, shows as finally inescapable the thought that the old
man has so long resisted—that every life is at last defeated by
time.

> 'My eyes are dim with childish tears,
> My heart is idly stirred,
> For the same sound is in my ears
> Which in those days I heard.'

The whole of this stanza suggests the unchanging reality against
which man measures his own change and decay. The old man's
eyes are 'dim' with tears like those of a child; with the 'vigorous
man' of the last stanza this gives the complete curve of life from
childhood, to maturity, and to old age. That his heart is 'idly
stirred' shows that Matthew recognizes his feelings as a mere
weakness; whatever he feels about his situation is irrelevant to
the forces that have produced it. The echo of his younger days in
the unchanging sound of the stream mocks his defeat. To make
all this explicit is to risk making it seem melodramatic; the art
consists largely in the quiet and apparently casual way in which
it is conveyed.

The next stanza is a model of compression and understatement:

> 'Thus fares it still in our decay:
> And yet the wiser mind
> Mourns less for what age takes away
> Than what it leaves behind.'

The immediate impression made by this is of an old man's trite
moralizing. What is said, however, is sharply in contrast with the
superficial tone. The note is one of resignation; 'thus fares it still
in our decay' accepts the common fate of man with a subdued
though fierce regret. This gives to the next line a deeper tone of
bitterness: what the 'wiser mind' will mourn for is not the loss of
vigour, health, and hope, but 'what it leaves behind'. What this
is remains unstated until later in the poem, so that the impression
is created of a pain that is too much for words. There is a deeply
ironical implication in 'the wiser mind'; man grows old and
learns wisdom so that he may apply it the better to his final
desolation.

There follows a statement in the simplest possible terms of the special burden that life lays on man. Unlike all other creatures he is 'pressed by heavy laws'. In accordance with the generally laconic style of the old man, these are not stated, although they are clearly the laws of time and change, and man's unhappy ability to recognize these laws; unlike the animals he knows hope and fear as well as memory and regret.

> 'The blackbird amid leafy trees,
> The lark above the hill,
> Let loose their carols when they please,
> Are quiet when they will.'

The blackbird 'amid leafy trees' suggests a protective sanctuary, the 'lark above the hill' a soaring unreflecting happiness; both these are denied to man. Even their being free to sing or be silent when they please has an ironic twist, because the old man is being asked to sing when he can scarcely speak for despair. Even the obligations of friendship may be too much when 'the grasshopper has become a burden'.

> 'With Nature never do *they* wage
> A foolish strife; they see
> A happy youth, and their old age
> Is beautiful and free.'

The birds are only of interest here because they define by contraries the condition of human life. The burden of consciousness lies on man as it does not on the animal kingdom; man alone feels anxiety for the future and regret for the past.

> 'But we are pressed by heavy laws;
> And often, glad no more,
> We wear a face of joy, because
> We have been glad of yore.'

Here Matthew dispels the illusion of cheerfulness in the old. If they seem to be happy, it is because earlier happiness, which in fact makes them the more wretched, has left them with the habit of appearing cheerful. Once again there is a deceptive and ironic contrast between the laconic manner and the bitterness of what is actually said, not about this old man alone, but about all human life when it is seen in its completed pattern.

In the next stanza 'what is left behind' is openly stated; the reserve on this point shown by the old man has made it seem almost too painful a thought for him to utter:

'If there be one who need bemoan
His kindred laid in earth,
The household hearts that were his own;
It is the man of mirth.'

The 'man of mirth' is at once the man who has known joy, and the singer of ballads, catches, and 'witty rhymes'—in short the poet, seen in imagination with the burden of a long life on him. This theme is returned to in 'Resolution and Independence', when the poet comes face to face with an 'old Man' who prefigures for him his own future. As in 'Resolution and Independence', the 'man of mirth' in this poem suffers more than others, since he has been more fully capable of love and joy.

The old man ends in despair:

'My days, my Friend, are almost gone,
My life has been approved,
And many love me! but by none
Am I enough beloved.'

These lines would be merely plaintive if they referred only to an individual old man. Matthew, however, speaks as the future self of the poet, when he has become 'approved' and loved of many, yet must himself be unknown except in his art. To the essential loneliness of every person is added the special loneliness of the poet.

This then is a poem written, like 'Resolution and Independence', to state not only the anxiety that the future arouses in all men, but in particular the anguish that faces the poet as he considers the 'gifts reserved for age'. The younger man offers to share the old man's burden:

'Now both himself and me he wrongs,
The man who thus complains!
I live and sing my idle songs
Upon these happy plains;

'And, Matthew, for thy children dead
I'll be a son to thee!'
At this he grasped my hand, and said,
'Alas! that cannot be.'

The young man, as a poet, is 'wronged' by this despair of the older 'man of mirth' and song, for of course he too is threatened by this vision of nothingness. He wishes only to sing his songs of innocence while he may, and to banish the spectre of Matthew's despair he offers to 'be a son' to him—to release him from his solitude and share his burden. The old man's answer—'Alas! that cannot be' is a quiet acceptance of the ultimate loneliness of the human mind.

The last lines of the poem achieve a dream-like and even ghostly quality; the movement from the fountain, and down the sheep-track to 'Leonard's rock' is described as a 'glide'—a motion that is possible to men only in dreams. The dream-like ease of the descent, like the 'bough of wilding' in 'The Two April Mornings', gives a visionary quality to the lines.

We rose up from the fountain-side;
And down the smooth descent
Of the green sheep-track did we glide;
And through the wood we went.

The gliding descent from the fountain, through the wood, and to the rock re-enacts in a trance-like motion the whole history of a man's life; the songs Matthew sings are an echo of his earlier merriment, a merriment that rings strangely hollow in the final defeat and isolation that he has acknowledged:

And, ere we came to Leonard's rock,
He sang those witty rhymes
About the crazy old church-clock,
And the bewildered chimes.

The last lines are an echo of the similar lines earlier in the poem, but they are emptied of all joy, and even tinged with madness. They conclude a poem in which Wordsworth has looked deep into the life of men and contemplated the final nothingness of existence. There is no offer of consolation in the poem, any more than there is in 'A slumber did my spirit seal'. Instead it offers, through Matthew's quiet and unself-pitying clarity, an image of the human courage that is needed to sustain the vision of ultimate defeat.

In spite of their appearance of simplicity, the 'Matthew' poems are both rigorous in thought and elaborate in structure. 'The Two April Mornings' ranges over a life-time by using a few carefully placed and sharply imagined incidents. An April morning remembered by the narrator serves to recall another April morning thirty years before which gave Matthew a view both of the past that had been lost and of the future that could not be. This penetration into the past enables the poet to provide a calculus of human joy and pain by which Matthew knows that nothing in the rest of his life can compensate for his loss. Finally, Matthew after his death is remembered as he was in the moment of recurrent grief. The death of Matthew's daughter echoes through the poem in a pattern of memories within memories. 'The Fountain' takes the calculation further, and reveals the necessary surplus of pain in human existence, which is always tormented by the consciousness of time. These poems represent an act of imaginative courage by which the poet looks at man's prospects when they are extended to a full life-time. The life of consciousness is dearly bought, but a poet may not allow himself to be unnerved. These poems show no trace of sentimentality, false comfort, or cynicism; they hold deep human sympathy and intellectual honesty in perfect balance.

5

THE 'LUCY' POEMS

In *Lyrical Ballads* Wordsworth set himself the task of showing that poetry could be written in 'the Language of conversation in the middle and lower classes of society'. In the volume that was published in 1798 most poems written in this style present some difficulty to the reader, either through the appearance of what seems to be absurdly matter-of-fact detail, or through the long-windedness of a tedious narrator. Although the strangeness and awkwardness of some of the details of such poems as 'The Thorn' and 'Simon Lee' may perhaps be accepted as a necessary part of the final poetic effect, there is no denying that the immediate impression they make is not favourable to a successful reading. To that extent it may be said that Wordsworth's experiment had not succeeded. He had won readers ready to admire his 'simplicity', but these were not prepared to look for much more; and the response of the literary critics was generally to treat such poems with contempt. It was only in the second edition of *Lyrical Ballads*, published in 1800, that poems appeared which, although not much more acceptable to contemporary cultivated taste than 'Simon Lee', yet achieve the aim that Wordsworth had in mind, without, for the most part, obtruding awkward matters of fact, and without the difficult repetitions usually associated with Wordsworth's narrators. The four 'Lucy' poems which appeared in the 1800 edition of *Lyrical Ballads* are worth careful attention, because they represent the clearest examples of the success of Wordsworth's experiment.

A good deal of attention has been given to the biographical problems raised by these poems. Who was Lucy? There is no answer to this question except to say that it is irrelevant. Lucy may or may not have been inspired by Dorothy Wordsworth, by Annette Vallon, or by another young woman. There is no reason to suppose that Wordsworth had any particular person in mind;

and whatever the nature of the personal experience behind them, these are not personal confessions. They are 'lyrical ballads', each of which tells a verse story and presents it dramatically. To confuse the mode of the 'Lucy' poems with that of the love lyric is to overlook their structure, in which, as in the traditional ballad, a story is told as boldly and briefly as possible, using dramatic changes of state, ironic inversions, and recognitions or 'discoveries'. They differ from the traditional ballad chiefly in the conscious intelligence which they bring to bear on man's condition, and in particular on the laws of nature with which all life must conform. It is the concentrated expression of this vision that gives rise to the powerful emotional response they command in the reader.

'Strange fits of passion' is more obviously a ballad than the other 'Lucy' poems. The narrator tells us that he has known 'strange fits of passion', that is to say, moments when strange fears have come into his mind. After asserting that a lover alone can understand what he is going to tell, he describes the journey he once made to 'Lucy's cot'. The story itself seems very simple. The lover rides on his journey, during which his eye is fixed on the moon, which, as he arrives at Lucy's cottage, suddenly disappears behind the cottage roof. The disappearance of the moon brings into the lover's mind an apparently irrational fear that Lucy may be dead:

> What fond and wayward thoughts will slide
> Into a Lover's head!
> 'O mercy!' to myself I cried,
> 'If Lucy should be dead!'

On a first reading it seems that this poem is concerned merely to show that lovers have foolish thoughts on very slight provocation. However, Wordsworth originally meant something rather different, for in the manuscript version there is an additional stanza which makes it clear that the lover's fear was later justified:

> I told her this; her laughter light
> Is ringing in my ears:
> And when I think upon that night
> My eyes are dim with tears.

Although this stanza was deleted from the final version, we must suppose that Wordsworth's intention was to give some validity to the apparently 'fond and foolish thought' by which the lover fears that Lucy may be dead.

If we now look more carefully at the poem, we shall see that it suggests two different ways of thinking about our lives in time. Usually we think of time as divisible into weeks, days, hours, minutes, and seconds; and we can therefore project into an indefinite future our own lives and the lives of others. The lover sees Lucy as existing from day to day, and does not normally think that sooner or later she must die:

> When she I loved looked every day
> Fresh as a rose in June,
> I to her cottage bent my way,
> Beneath an evening-moon.

The comparison with the rose, which blossoms in June only to fade soon after, offers an ironic comment on the complacency of the lover's view of Lucy, whom he sees 'every day' blossoming like a rose, but of whom he does not usually allow himself to think that she must sooner or later fade. The hint is made more strongly with the introduction of an 'evening-moon'—in other words a moon that is about to set. When the lover says that 'all the while' he kept his eyes upon the descending moon he is ironically unaware of what he is saying. He sees the moon sinking, but at the same time he thinks of Lucy as a rose that will go on blooming 'every day'.

The lover continues his story, and as he does so he illustrates the way in which we eagerly move forward through clock-time, without realizing that every step forward through time brings us nearer to an end:

> Upon the moon I fixed my eye,
> All over the wide lea;
> With quickening pace my horse drew nigh
> Those paths so dear to me.

Here the lover, though watching the moon descending, is not aware that it is doing so. For him time is represented by the

'quickening pace' of his horse towards the object of his desire. In
the next stanza the drama is heightened:

> And now we reached the orchard-plot;
> And, as we climbed the hill,
> The sinking moon to Lucy's cot
> Came near, and nearer still.

The slow descent of the moon—'near, and nearer still'—towards
Lucy's cot suggests the approach of a threat. But still the lover
has not consciously learned the lesson that the moon is about to
convey to him. The reason for this, as the poet now suggests, is
that we find it intolerably painful to think of time as a process by
which all living things move through decay to their deaths. We
prefer the clock-time with which we are familiar, and which we
can imagine as being extended indefinitely into the future:

> In one of those sweet dreams I slept,
> Kind Nature's gentlest boon!
> And all the while my eyes I kept
> On the descending moon.

The repetition of the 'evening-moon', the 'sinking moon', and
now the 'descending moon' creates an insistent pattern of
suggestion which, because of his natural resistance to such
awareness, the lover ignores. He continues his journey in uncon-
sciousness of what is being presented before his very eyes. At the
same time the steady rise and fall of his horse's hooves marks off
the beat of clock-time, and contrasts by its intermittent nature
with the slow and inexorable descent of the moon. It is at this
moment that the moon disappears entirely, and thus forces to the
lover's mind the consciousness of what has been enacted:

> My horse moved on; hoof after hoof
> He raised, and never stopped:
> When down behind the cottage roof
> At once, the bright moon dropped.

With this sudden disappearance of the moon the curve of its
motion across the sky—imperceptible until it cuts the horizon
and disappears—is dramatically revealed. The speed with which it
vanishes is not in itself mysterious; Wordsworth is always
careful with such details. The rotation of the earth, causing the

moon to set, and the lover's closer approach to the cottage on the hill, which cuts the moon from his view as it sets, account sufficiently for the sudden vanishing. When this happens, the lover suddenly fears that Lucy may be dead, because in a flash of intuition, he realizes that the 'rose in June' is fated to die as surely as the moon is fated to set. We do not think of the moon as it shines in the sky as 'setting' or of a rose in full bloom as 'dying', but if we remember that life is process, and not the movement of an unchanging object through clock-time, we realize that the moon's setting is implied in its shining, and that death is implied in life. This notion of the curve of life is stated more directly in the 'Mutability' sonnet:

> From low to high doth dissolution climb,
> And sink from high to low, along a scale
> Of awful notes, whose concord shall not fail;
> A musical but melancholy chime.

The lover's fear, although it is not immediately shown to be well founded, is no 'fond and foolish thought', in spite of his desire to believe this. In the original version Wordsworth made this plain in the additional stanza telling us of the lover's 'tears' when he looks back on that night. What the lover experiences is a moment of shocking realization of a truth that can be faced only briefly—that all life, including Lucy's, is a pattern in which growth and decay form a single process, the end of which is certain. Lucy, like the rose and the moon, is, after all, subject to the 'touch of earthly years'.

'Three years she grew in sun and shower' also tells a story, most of which is narrated by Nature herself. This is the story of the growth of Lucy to mature beauty, and the process by which this beauty is achieved. As in 'Strange fits of passion', Lucy is thought of as a flower:

> Three years she grew in sun and shower,
> Then Nature said, 'A lovelier flower
> On earth was never sown;
> This Child I to myself will take;
> She shall be mine, and I will make
> A Lady of my own.'

There is perhaps no need to make an elaborate mystery of Nature's choice of Lucy. It presumably means only that the poem deals with one of Nature's favourites, a young woman upon whom she showers her greatest benefits of grace and beauty. The promise that Nature makes is to produce an almost perfect woman, and in doing so she reveals the methods by which she works to create the complex unity of a living being. Wordsworth shows a recurrent interest in the emergence of organic forms of life from the brute matter and the simple forces of the physical universe. In the poem the process is one of opposing polarities, of a dialectic from which the living complexity arises:

> Myself will to my darling be
> Both law and impulse: and with me
> The Girl, in rock and plain,
> In earth and heaven, in glade and bower,
> Shall feel an overseeing power
> To kindle or restrain.

The whole of this passage is marked by a pattern of antitheses, between 'law and impulse', 'rock and plain', 'earth and heaven', 'glade and bower' and 'kindle' and 'restrain'. These opposing principles are the loom in which the elaborate fabric of life is woven.

The next stanza deals with the vital energy produced by this opposition of forces:

> She shall be sportive as the fawn
> That wild with glee across the lawn
> Or up the mountain springs;
> And hers shall be the breathing balm,
> And hers the silence and the calm
> Of mute insensate things.

If we imagine too definitely a particular Lucy leaping up the mountain or springing 'wild with glee across the lawn' a somewhat ludicrous picture emerges. But if the poem is being read with attention to its real subject, this question scarcely arises. Lucy is not a particular person so much as the representative of all organic living beings. In all life, the capacity for calm rest and deep sleep, for contemplation and quiet, depends upon the opposite principle of energy and joy. So the vital energy of Lucy is a condition without which she could not enjoy

> . . . the silence and the calm
> Of mute insensate things.

Lucy's being is moulded not only by physical forces, but also by her imagination, which can respond to the patterns which she perceives in the universe. Not only the more obviously graceful forms of nature, like the bending willow, but even the 'motions of the Storm' may be converted by the perceiving imagination into perspicuous patterns and models for the human life itself. Lucy shall not 'fail to see':

> The floating clouds their state shall lend
> To her; for her the willow bend;
> Nor shall she fail to see
> Even in the motions of the Storm
> Grace that shall mould the Maiden's form
> By silent sympathy.

Wordsworth of course understood very well that the world is largely what the perceiving mind makes of it, and we are not to suppose here a simple-minded notion of human life as moulded by external forms without its own active participation. This is also evident in the stanza that follows, where the maiden must listen and be attentive if she is to find in Nature the harmony which is to be reflected in her own being:

> The stars of midnight shall be dear
> To her; and she shall lean her ear
> In many a secret place
> Where rivulets dance their wayward round,
> And beauty born of murmuring sound
> Shall pass into her face.

Here two opposing principles are once again advanced, the eternal order of the stars of midnight, and the ever-changing dance of the rivulets. Once again Wordsworth expresses his sense of wonder at the complex inter-relationships between the permanent and unchanging laws of nature, and the magical complexities which they produce, complexities which include not only the dancing rivulets, but also such phenomena as beautiful young women.

These then are the processes by which, as Nature says, she will rear Lucy's form 'to stately height'. We are again reminded that Lucy is not being passively moulded by Nature, for she is given 'such thoughts' by Nature as part of the whole process:

Part of process is having imposed feelings.

> And vital feelings of delight
> Shall rear her form to stately height,
> Her virgin bosom swell;
> Such thoughts to Lucy I will give
> While she and I together live
> Here in this happy dell.

The dramatic inversion, so characteristic of these ballads, now occurs:

> Thus Nature spake—The work was done—
> How soon my Lucy's race was run!
> She died, and left to me
> This heath, this calm, and quiet scene;
> The memory of what has been,
> And never more will be.

Universal

The final stanza with its reversal of expectations and its sudden intrusion of Lucy's death gives a poignant ending to the poem. The joyful creation of life has as its inevitable result the creating ☆ of death. This again is not merely a lament over the death of a particular young woman called Lucy. It is a statement of the condition of all human life, in which all the powers of nature combine in complex ways to create a human being, which is doomed by nature's law to death. Here we may compare Wilfred Owen's poem 'Futility' in which an officer looking at a dead soldier asks whether the process of creation is worth the trouble:

> O what made fatuous sunbeams toil
> To break earth's sleep at all?

There is, however, in Wordsworth's poem, for all its poignancy and its dramatic force, little querulousness or rebellion. The tragic force of this short dramatic poem relies upon an account of the natural processes at work, and makes no direct appeal to our sentiments. We are for that reason all the more deeply moved. When the whole elaborate process of life is over there is nothing. The quiet movement of the last lines carries with it an unusual clarity of perception. The lover makes no complaint, expresses no grief, he merely states that there is nothing left but a memory, which by its very existence deepens the sense of loss:

> She died, and left to me
> This heath, this calm, and quiet scene;
> The memory of what has been,
> And never more will be.

Like 'Strange fits of passion have I known', this 'Lucy' poem is concerned not merely with a particular person, but with a universal truth about human life, a truth so commonplace and yet so painful that we live with it always and yet rarely recognize it. The power of such poems lies in their capacity to awaken a knowledge that is theoretically known to us but which usually we do not care to apply imaginatively to our own lives.

The third poem of this series to be considered is 'A slumber did my spirit seal', a poem in which Wordsworth achieves an even greater dramatic compression than in those we have examined. This poem consists of two stanzas only, and the dramatic inversion comes at the end of the first stanza. Once again the poet is concerned with the condition of unknowing, of refusing to realize the truth about existence:

> A slumber did my spirit seal;
>   I had no human fears:
> She seemed a thing that could not feel
>   The touch of earthly years.
>
> No motion has she now, no force;
>   She neither hears nor sees;
> Rolled round in earth's diurnal course,
>   With rocks, and stones, and trees.

The first stanza quietly prepares for the dramatic reversal of the second stanza, and the awakening, or recognition, that accompanies it. As in 'Strange fits of passion', the lover lives—as men habitually do—in a 'slumber' of the mind, with the gates of perception closed. Though not a 'thing', Lucy is thought of as having the relative permanence of a *thing*, not as an organic growth which from its very nature must fade and die within determined limits of time. The lover has 'no human fears'; his serenity is either god-like, or less than human, but in either case it is a refusal to accept the condition of being fully human and mortal, and the lover of a mortal woman. The lover's spiritual slumber takes account of the 'touch of earthly years' only to invest his Lucy with a special immunity; as if she was not, like other mortals, subject to time:

> She seemed a thing that could not feel
> The touch of earthly years.

There is here a suggestion that the sealing of the lover's spirit is a kind of *hubris*. He has exempted himself and his Lucy from the common lot of man, and of all living things; and his awakening is ironically implied in the very description of his slumber.

The reversal and recognition come with a dramatic force unequalled in the other 'Lucy' poems. The second stanza reveals that Lucy has indeed become a *thing*, and it does so in terms that enforce the sense of utter loss, but at the same time achieve a kind of reconciliation. There are very few examples of so much being said in so few words. The notion of Lucy as a 'thing', so lightly touched on in the first stanza, is now enforced with the implacable authority of the whole universe. She has the status of a *thing*, in being incapable of motion and utterly insentient. She is 'rolled round' with the earth in its daily rotation, which in its turn is made a mere passive conforming with the whole vast machinery of the universe by the use of the word 'diurnal'—a technical term in astronomy. That she is 'rolled round' also suggests that she is like a stone or rock that can be 'rolled', as the earth, while turning on its axis, is itself 'rolled round' the sun. The last line—'With rocks, and stones, and trees'—comes like a series of hammer-blows, creating an impressive effect of finality. The lover now sees Lucy as a thing among other things, all of them subject to the same laws. The special status granted to her by the lover's heart was an illusion.

This widening of the context to the inorganic and the organic world as a whole—'rocks, and stones, and trees'—brings with it, however, even in the moment of awakening to a bitter truth, a reconciliation, or at least something of the calm that comes from having faced the truth. The whole of the last stanza—in which the word 'diurnal', amongst so many simple and common words, plays a key role—suggests that Lucy's death is in accordance with the laws of the universe, which, however implacable, is magnificently organized. Like Job, the poet can submit himself to an order which commands his admiration. Wordsworth could still feel the wonder expressed by Addison at the Newtonian order:

> What though, in solemn silence, all
> Move round the dark terrestrial ball?
> What though nor real voice nor sound
> Amid their radiant orbs be found?
> In Reason's ear they all rejoice,
> And utter forth a glorious voice,
> For ever singing, as they shine,
> The Hand that made us is Divine.

Wordsworth's acceptance is muted; there is no longer the same fresh enthusiasm for the laws of the universe as revealed by science, nor so much open piety. But Newton and Newton's laws still have the power to strengthen the poet's sanity, for they announce an order which, however implacable, is never arbitrary, and imposes its rule with all the majesty of eternal law. The balance achieved in this poem between pain and acceptance is not, for Wordsworth, a precarious one; but it could probably have been achieved at no other time in history.

'She dwelt among the untrodden ways' also tells the story of Lucy's growth, perfection, and death. Once again Lucy is thought of as a flower—'A violet by a mossy stone'—and once again the whole story is told with great compression and intensity:

> She dwelt among the untrodden ways
>   Beside the springs of Dove,
> A Maid whom there were none to praise
>   And very few to love:
>
> A violet by a mossy stone
>   Half hidden from the eye!
> —Fair as a star, when only one
>   Is shining in the sky.

> She lived unknown, and few could know
>   When Lucy ceased to be;
> But she is in her grave, and, oh,
>   The difference to me!

Lucy as an obscure flower, a violet, is shown as having dwelt, like a violet, in an unfrequented place. It seems that what Wordsworth means is that Lucy dwells 'Beside the springs of Dove', that is to say, in a deep and shady place. The River Dove runs its early course through a deep and rocky dale, providing an apt equivalent for the shady obscurity in which a violet grows.

The point that is made most insistently in the first two stanzas is that Lucy, though beautiful, is valued by very few. And here we must note that she is compared, not only with that most retiring flower, the violet, but with the most public beauty that is possible—that of a single star when it is shining in the sky. Some critics comment on the sexlessness of Lucy in this poem. But she is compared here with the star which is usually seen shining when 'only one' is visible, the planet Venus, star of the goddess of love. And it is as well to note that Wordsworth's original version suggests some interest in Lucy's physical attractions:

> My hope was one, from cities far,
> Nursed on a lonesome heath;
> Her lips were red as roses are,
> Her hair a woodbine wreath.

The last stanza, continuing the pattern of antitheses so usual in these 'Lucy' poems, contrasts the general indifference to Lucy's life and death with the sense of loss felt by the narrator. For the great majority of people, her death means nothing. For the few who do know her she has simply 'ceased to be'. But one person at least has felt her death as a numbing loss. No direct statement is made of this in the last two lines; but its very phrasing, the exclamation at the end of the line—as though wrenched out of the speaker by pain—and the lack of any attempt to find an exact equivalent for the speaker's grief, all combine to give a strictly dramatic sense of the speaker's loss.

The structure once again is cyclical. The 'springs of Dove'

suggest the origins of life, the 'violet by a mossy stone' its emergence from brute matter. Lucy, we are told, 'lived unknown' —the story of her life completed in two words—and has 'ceased to be'. Now 'she is in her grave', and the circle is closed. The 'mossy stone' from which the violet springs is also the stone over its grave. In the original version, the process of growth and decay—a constant theme of these poems—was made more explicitly:

> And she was graceful as the broom
> That flowers by Carron's side;
> But slow distemper checked her bloom,
> And on the heath she died.

The omission of this stanza greatly strengthened the poem, by concentrating attention on the violet, and by increasing the dramatic compression. The cancelled stanza is interesting, however, because it makes clearer what is lightly suggested in the poem in its final form—that Lucy's memory is precious partly because, like the violet and the 'broom', she had died where her roots are—'on the heath she died'. The circle is completed quietly, with 'Lucy ceased to be'; there is not much to be felt about this, any more than when a flower dies.

So far all has been as it would be if seen by an almost indifferent stranger. It is only in the last two lines that a dramatic change, and a recognition, is achieved with a sudden shift in the point of view. To one who loved her, Lucy—who has not 'disturbed the universe'—is immeasurably valuable; and though her death makes no difference to the world, it makes an inexpressible difference to one person. The poignancy of this recognition is increased by the isolation of the mourner; grief is all the harder to bear because it is not shared, and because there is no reason why it should be shared. The isolation is accepted as natural, and there is no protest against what must be. The lover is, however, left at the end contemplating his knowledge that all that is left of Lucy is the grief he feels for her; otherwise she is nothing, and has made no difference to the world.

This apparently simple poem contains within itself a part of the revolution in thought that was taking place in Wordsworth's time. The poet Gray in his 'Elegy in a Country Churchyard' considers that there are many humble and obscure persons who, with better opportunities, might have become famous and highly valued. What this poem asserts, however, is that value has nothing to do with public judgment. The individual mind may create its own value, and Lucy is no less fair, and no less loved, although she is valued by one person only. This is a firm assertion of the validity of subjective judgments of value—a belief held at no time with more assurance and firmness than in Wordsworth's day. This is not to say that Wordsworth is not conscious of the difference between private values and public valuation. The difference between the violet and the star is a measure of that. However, the preference for the individual and private value over public judgment is conveyed strongly by the imagery of the second stanza, in which the violet is more attractive because more vital than the star. This may of course be read merely as a story of the narrator's grief for a beautiful country girl; but then much of the intelligence that Wordsworth put into it is lost.

'I travelled among unknown men' was written in 1801, two years after the other poems in the group. It resembles the others in telling the story of Lucy's life and death, but this story is here prefaced with two stanzas in which the narrator describes his return after foreign travel to the scenes he associates with Lucy:

> I travelled among unknown men,
>   In lands beyond the sea;
> Nor, England! did I know till then
>   What love I bore to thee.
>
> 'Tis past, that melancholy dream!
>   Nor will I quit thy shore
> A second time; for still I seem
>   To love thee more and more.

These first stanzas are a necessary prelude to what follows, when the traveller returns to the security of England, the mountains, and the memory of Lucy, to the known and the familiar. The last stanzas suggest that only 'natural piety'—a reliance on what the mind has grown with—can give solidity and 'reality' to our experience. The travelling among 'unknown men' in countries which are not mentioned by name, but are merely 'lands beyond the sea', has been a 'melancholy dream', since what the imagination cannot fully organize is not fully real. The love of England is a love of imaginative order. There is no metaphysical terror as in the Simplon Pass, and no great moral struggle, no revolutionary war, to impede the search for 'order and relation'.

> Among thy mountains did I feel
>   The joy of my desire;
> And she I cherished turned her wheel
>   Beside an English fire.
>
> Thy mornings showed, thy nights concealed,
>   The bowers where Lucy played;
> And thine too is the last green field,
>   That Lucy's eyes surveyed.

The narrator's return to the scene of his earlier love is a return to the order of a pattern which, although it involves loss and pain, is yet familiar and therefore to some degree reassuring. The history of Lucy as it is told here is firmly cyclical; the spinning-wheel that Lucy turns beside 'an English fire' dominates the last part of the poem, in which she is shown as moving through a cycle of childhood, maturity, and death. The sense of return to a known and familiar pattern is so strong in this poem that it makes the story of Lucy seem predetermined and yet not painful. The turning of the wheel of day and night, youth and age, beside the hearth and within the security of the mountains, speaks of a protective, encircling order. The love of Lucy has been fostered in England, among the mountains, and Lucy herself has lived through the recurring days and nights by the encircling 'bowers' in which she played as a child. Her death is not mentioned, but only implied, as though she has gently completed the turning of the wheel; moreover, it is implied in an image of rest and peace, and a suggestion of the Psalmist's words: 'He maketh me to lie down in green pastures':

> And thine too is the last green field,
>   That Lucy's eyes surveyed.

This is of course in one sense a love story, but it is also an account of the natural piety by which Wordsworth increasingly believed it necessary to live. The restlessness of foreign travel led him to value familiar places, familiar patterns, and a natural inter-connection of all the various parts of experience. This poem marks a distinct decline from the tragic perception and intellectual energy of the other 'Lucy' poems. It shows the beginning of the tendency to seek for 'a repose that ever is the same' that slowly led Wordsworth's poetic powers to decline. This is not to say that the poem is without value. On the contrary, it expresses with quiet assurance the value of a life lived within the protective circle of a national and social tradition.

6

'MICHAEL'

Wordsworth wrote a number of narrative poems, in styles varying from the bald and homely language of 'Simon Lee' to the classical decorum and the Virgilian cadences of 'Laodamia'. There is space here for the consideration of only one of these poems, and I have chosen 'Michael' because it is one of the most successful, uniting purity of language and directness of style with a decorum and firmness which may properly be called classical.

The poem is described by Wordsworth as a 'pastoral'. This should be noticed, because it seems intended to remind us that the humble life of Michael is not to be taken as the kind of realism that we find, for example, in the poetry of Crabbe. On the contrary, the poem deals with the condition of human life, of which Michael is a representative, chosen because in his isolation as a shepherd and among the hills he has an elemental dignity.

The poem begins with an invitation to the reader to turn from the 'public way' and walk upstream along the 'tumultuous brook of Green-head Ghyll'. In such 'bold ascent', the poet tells us, 'your feet must struggle' because the 'pastoral mountains front you, face to face'. This opening is not to be taken as merely local colour. It states the theme of the poem, which is concerned with man's endless struggle against the forces that pull him down and sooner or later reduce all life to a dead level. The narrator continues:

> But, courage! for around that boisterous brook
> The mountains have all opened out themselves,
> And made a hidden valley of their own.
> No habitation can be seen; but they
> Who journey thither find themselves alone
> With a few sheep, with rocks and stones, and kites
> That overhead are sailing in the sky.

(6–12)

76

This 'hidden valley' is the world in which Michael dwells. The 'few sheep', the 'rocks and stones', suggest the austere conditions of Michael's life; there is, however, a further and more sinister touch in the 'kites' that fly over the scene, since this reminds the reader of the shadow of death that hangs over the valley, the sheep, and the shepherd himself. This scene, as Wordsworth tells us, is 'in truth an utter solitude'. The poet now draws attention to an object which, as he says, one might easily fail to notice:

> Beside the brook
> Appears a straggling heap of unhewn stones!
>
> (16–17)

This is the object which is the occasion of the story. In a manuscript version the following passage is to be found:

> There is a shapeless crowd of unhewn stones
> That lie together, some in heaps, and some
> In lines, that seem to keep themselves alive
> In the last dotage of a dying form.

(*Poetical Works of William Wordsworth*, ed. E. de Selincourt and H. Darbishire, 5 vols., Oxford University Press, 1940–9, II, 482)

In this manuscript version Wordsworth makes clear what is only strongly hinted at in the poem—that the 'straggling heap of unhewn stones'—all that now remains of the sheepfold Michael is building in the poem—are themselves a representation of man's life. The 'dotage of a dying form' links the process by which the forces of wind, sun, and gravity cause the collapse of the wall with the more elaborate but equally inexorable forces which reduce man himself to dotage and finally to death. What this poem is concerned with, then, is the process of dissolution, and the reducing of man's achievement and his very life to shapelessness and disintegration. It is a story of man's struggle to maintain himself and his values in a hostile universe. As Wordsworth says, this tale of Michael, heard when he was a boy, led him to feel for other men and to think

> On man, the heart of man, and human life.
>
> (33)

He therefore undertakes to tell this history even though it be 'homely and rude'.

The tale itself begins with a description of the shepherd. He is described as an old man who is 'stout of heart, and strong of limb'. The whole process of his life is briefly laid before the reader:

> His bodily frame had been from youth to age
> Of an unusual strength: his mind was keen,
> Intense, and frugal, apt for all affairs,
> And in his shepherd's calling he was prompt
> And watchful more than ordinary men.
>
> (42–6)

Michael has not been an unconscious peasant, but has 'learned the meaning of all winds'. The storms, for him, are not a reason for seeking refuge, but a summons 'up to the mountains'. He has been 'amid the heart of many thousand mists'. In other words, Michael represents man at his most adventurous, courageous, and conscious. The valleys, streams, and rocks, the fields and hills among which he had lived, have, says the poet, 'laid Strong hold on his affections': they are to him

> A pleasurable feeling of blind love,
> The pleasure which there is in life itself.
>
> (76–7)

This whole introductory passage serves to make of Michael a representative of man's struggle and of man's consciousness. The mountains, hills, and streams which surround him are not merely objects of local interest. They are the representation of the world in which man exists, and in which he struggles to realize himself and the life that is within him. We begin now to see that Wordsworth is here creating a new Adam, destined to live not in a paradise, but in a nature as it presented itself to an imagination nourished on the science of the eighteenth century. This universe, in which all life is subjected to fixed laws which must sooner or later bring about its end, is one in which it is not easy for man to live. For this reason Michael is presented as a heroic figure, who may suggest to us how best we can maintain our lives in the context of the physical universe, and how man himself gives significance and value to the world he inhabits.

As one would expect, there must be an Eve for Wordsworth's Adam. In the next passage Wordsworth introduces Michael's wife. Just as Michael himself is made representative of man, so his wife follows the traditional occupations of a woman—those associated with her in Homer and ever since. She has two wheels 'of antique form', one for spinning wool, and one for spinning flax; and these wheels are alternately put to work. They have an only child, whose function in the poem is to be a successor to Michael. For this reason we are told that he was born when Michael began to feel that he was old, and to have 'one foot in the grave'. He is, for the same reason, an 'only son'. The life of the family is described as a round of humble tasks, all of them playing their part in sustaining life against the assaults that nature makes on it.

If there were any doubt that Michael, his wife, and his son are meant as universally representative figures, the passage that follows would remove it. The cottage is described in terms which suggest the world itself:

> Down from the ceiling, by the chimney's edge,
> That in our ancient uncouth country style
> With huge and black projection over-browed
> Large space beneath, as duly as the light
> Of day grew dim the Housewife hung a lamp;
> An aged utensil, which had performed
> Service beyond all others of its kind.
>
> (110–16)

Here the cottage with its great fireplace is made to suggest the vastness of the world, in which the housewife hangs a lamp that shines out to the ends of space:

> For, as it chanced,
> Their cottage on a plot of rising ground
> Stood single, with large prospect, north and south,
> High into Easedale, up to Dunmail-Raise,
> And westward to the village near the lake;
> And from this constant light, so regular,
> And so far seen, the House itself, by all

Who dwelt within the limits of the vale,
Both old and young, was named THE EVENING STAR.

(131–9)

The lamp lit by the housewife as darkness falls is an 'aged utensil' which has performed 'Service beyond all others of its kind'. The shining out of this lamp like a star makes Michael and his cottage into a centre of light in the surrounding darkness, as man provides a centre of consciousness within nature. The lamp is lit 'duly' each evening as the light of day grows dim; the act is almost a ritual, celebrating the continual renewal of man's intellectual life in a world where it is the sole source of light.

In the next passage we are told of Michael's love for his 'Helpmate', and we are also told that the 'son of his old age' was even more dear to him. The reason given is that above all the gifts 'That earth can offer to declining man' a son is the most important because he brings the hope of a continuance of life when man himself 'by tendency of nature needs must fail'. For this reason Michael is shown as tenderly giving a woman's care to his son. The boldness of this passage succeeds entirely; we are made to feel through Michael's 'acts of tenderness' the desperate need that he has for another life to take over when his own inevitably fails:

Exceeding was the love he bare to him,
His heart and his heart's joy! For oftentimes
Old Michael, while he was a babe in arms,
Had done him female service, not alone
For pastime and delight, as is the use
Of fathers, but with patient mind enforced
To acts of tenderness; and he had rocked
His cradle, as with a woman's gentle hand.

(151–8)

The description of the 'large old oak' that follows is on the surface merely an elaboration of anecdotal detail. However, the appearance of this aged tree, figuring endurance against the forces of time and decay, adds a further suggestion of man's own struggle. It is under the Tree of Life that the old man instructs his child in the art of shearing sheep:

There, while they two were sitting in the shade,
With others round them, earnest all and blithe,
Would Michael exercise his heart with looks
Of fond correction and reproof bestowed
Upon the Child, if he disturbed the sheep
By catching at their legs, or with his shouts
Scared them, while they lay still beneath the shears.

(170–6)

The next object described is the staff which Michael 'from a winter coppice cut' and formed into a 'perfect shepherd's staff'. This he gives to the boy so that he may be equipped to guard the flock. This, we must remember, is a pastoral poem; and the fashioning of the shepherd's staff and its presentation to the boy are to be taken as something more than rustic anecdote. Michael is presenting the staff to the son almost as a ritual gesture, and in doing so is passing on the task of guarding the sheep. And so we learn that as the boy grows up 'the old Man's heart seemed born again'.

He with his Father daily went, and they
Were as companions, why should I relate
That objects which the Shepherd loved before
Were dearer now? that from the Boy there came
Feelings and emanations—things which were
Light to the sun and music to the wind;
And that the old Man's heart seemed born again?

(197–203)

Michael now falls on evil days, and is called upon to discharge a debt which he has guaranteed. He is faced with the threat of having to sell a portion of his 'patrimonial fields'. He therefore resolves, since the loss of the fields would be for Michael an equivalent to betrayal in any other profession or trade, to send his son to work for a kinsman in the city. This prospect fills the mind of Michael and his wife with new hope. Other young men have gone to the city and have prospered and grown 'wondrous rich', and the pair are so delighted at the prospect that they announce that 'If he *could* go, the Boy should go tonight'. This is their immediate feeling; but Michael begins to be 'troubled in his sleep', and one morning the housewife could see 'that all his hopes were gone'. Michael knows in his heart that the abandoning of the established pattern of life can only lead to a destruction of all his hopes. His wife perceives this, and in a passage of biblical strength she declares to Luke:

> 'Thou must not go:
> We have no other Child but thee to lose,
> None to remember—do not go away,
> For if thou leave thy Father he will die.'
>
> (295–8)

This momentary perception of the truth is, however, dissipated by the youth's self-assurance; the original plan is cheerfully returned to, and the boy departs for the city.

The parting of father and son takes place by the 'heap of stones' which Michael had gathered by the edge of the stream in preparation for the building of a stone-walled sheepfold. The choice of this place is of course deliberate; the task of Michael is represented by the heap of stones, and the force of time against which he struggles in vain is represented by the stream. Here Michael briefly tells his son the story of their own lives, insisting on the deep and abiding link between them, and claiming by implication the son's loyalty and his devotion to the continuing task:

> —Even to the utmost I have been to thee
> A kind and a good Father: and herein
> I but repay a gift which I myself
> Received at others' hands; for, though now old
> Beyond the common life of man, I still
> Remember them who loved me in my youth.
> Both of them sleep together: here they lived,
> As all their Forefathers had done; and, when
> At length their time was come, they were not loth
> To give their bodies to the family mould.
>
> (361–70)

At this point Michael asks Luke to lay one stone of the sheepfold with his own hands. This symbolic act is meant to commit Luke to the task that his father has begun. He is to go away but is to remain faithful to the purpose for which he has been destined. Luke is to lay the corner-stone as a symbol of the 'natural piety' to which his father wishes to bind him. Luke lays the corner-stone, the father weeps over him, and he departs for the city.

At first all is well, and the shepherd goes cheerfully about his tasks, including the building of the sheepfold. But Luke begins to 'slacken in his duty' and we are very briefly, indeed almost abruptly, told that 'in the dissolute city' he followed 'evil courses' and was driven to hide beyond the seas. There is no suggestion here of any particular moral, or of condemnation of the son for his wickedness or of the shepherd for his misjudgment. What is involved here, it seems, is a tragic recognition of what follows when the established patterns of life are broken. Wordsworth describes in 'Residence in London', in *The Prelude*, the state of affairs in the city where man is utterly disconnected from man, and the order of natural piety is destroyed. What is presented in 'Residence in London' as a nightmare is here presented as tragedy. Man, as he is represented by Michael, a figure sustained by tradition and by the dignity of his task, is threatened not merely with the failure of his hopes, but with extinction as a type. Just as the old man is unable to complete the building of the sheepfold, but must leave the unfinished wall to collapse into a 'shapeless heap of stones', so the ordered life of man seems destined, under the pressure of change, to be broken up into disconnectedness and chaos. It is not the tragedy of Michael only that is here portrayed, but the tragedy of man.

The old man is shown as responding to his misfortune with an elemental strength and dignity:

> Among the rocks
> He went, and still looked up to sun and cloud,
> And listened to the wind; and, as before,
> Performed all kinds of labour for his sheep,
> And for the land, his small inheritance.
> And to that hollow dell from time to time
> Did he repair, to build the Fold of which
> His flock had need. 'Tis not forgotten yet
> The pity which was then in every heart
> For the old Man—and 'tis believed by all
> That many and many a day he thither went,
> And never lifted up a single stone.

(455–66)

The quietness of this passage is extraordinarily impressive. The old man performs his tasks as before, caring for his sheep and for his land. He goes, moreover, to the dell to build the sheepfold, but this is a task which he can no longer continue. The suggestion of heartbreak and ultimate defeat in spite of an enduring courage is beautifully achieved. The whole of the poem is focused in one quietly tragic line:

> And never lifted up a single stone.

In this line is expressed the ultimate defeat of Michael's life, not only by the fact which he has already accepted, that he must sooner or later be physically incapable of struggling against the weight of things, but in the much more deeply felt defeat through the breaking of the bond of natural piety, and the loss of the son who was to have continued his task.

The suggestion of a desolation that far exceeds the individual story of Michael is clearly conveyed in the final paragraph. The old man sits by the sheepfold with his faithful dog, leaving the work of building unfinished, and so he dies. Isabel, we are told, survived her husband for three years or little more, and

> at her death the estate
> Was sold, and went into a stranger's hand.
>
> (474–5)

The deaths of Michael and Isabel are in themselves a part of the natural order. The son's defection, the sequestration of the estate, and the intrusion of the 'stranger's hand', however, mark a breach of that order. The poem continues:

> The Cottage which was named the Evening Star
> Is gone—the ploughshare has been through the ground
> On which it stood; great changes have been wrought
> In all the neighbourhood:—yet the oak is left
> That grew beside their door; and the remains
> Of the unfinished Sheep-fold may be seen
> Beside the boisterous brook of Greenhead Ghyll.
>
> (476–82)

In this passage the suggestion is of the extinguishing of the Evening Star, the light which shone from Michael's cottage into widest space. The suggestion of a final defeat is conveyed in a traditional metaphor; the ploughshare has gone through the ground. The 'great changes' are not only in a humble cottage and its surroundings, but in the very life they represent. This poem, with its biblical overtones and its pastoral manner, is apocalyptic in tone and intention. It prefigures the collapse of a society, and it does so through a system of images—the stone and the stream—which make the defeat of any particular form of life a part of the very law of the universe. Yet the poem ends with a suggestion of faith in the ultimate powers of life. The oak remains that grew beside Michael's door, and life continues, even though of Michael and his struggle there is left only the pathetic evidence of the 'unfinished Sheep-fold' by the side of the stream.

Wordsworth has succeeded in turning the story of an obscure shepherd into a deeply moving poem which touches on concerns that are felt by all. His account of the shepherd and his task is utterly without condescension. Michael is represented as a fellow-man, like all men seeking to create an area of order and harmony around him, and like all men looking to a new generation to carry on the task. The identification of feeling is complete; Wordsworth himself, in telling the tale, says that he does so 'for the delight of a few natural hearts'; but also

> for the sake
> Of youthful Poets, who among the hills
> Will be my second self when I am gone.

$(37-9)$

In this way Wordsworth as a poet asserts his common feeling with Michael, for both are engaged in the task of sustaining life, and both are dependent on the hope that their task will be continued. The link between the poet and the shepherd is made with quiet mastery in the description of the giving to the boy of the shepherd's staff. This takes full account of the human realities; the 'urchin' is too young to help his father much, and is 'something between a hindrance and a help'. But this in itself serves to stress the symbolical nature of the gift; it is an initiation into his father's trade rather than an apprenticeship. The hooping of the staff with iron suggests the rigour that all commitment involves; and the guarding of the sheep is made significant of the inescapable duty that manhood lays upon us:

> He as a watchman oftentimes was placed
> At gate or gap, to stem or turn the flock.
>
> (185–6)

The vigilant young watchman evokes the contrasting recollection of the 'blind mouths' in Milton's 'Lycidas', where the unworthy shepherds 'scarce know how to hold A sheephook', and betray their flock to the wolves. The appeal to the 'natural heart' is direct and strong; there is a deep pathos in the picture of the 'urchin' taking on the responsibilities of a man. But this is no mere sentimentality about humble life; the law that asks in the name of natural piety for each generation to take over the burden in its turn is one that applies to shepherd and poet alike, to Milton and to Wordsworth, and to all who share in the life of responsibility.

Wordsworth is not concerned only with the results of courage and devotion; the hills in which Michael works are a challenge to the exercise of qualities that themselves give value to life:

> Fields, where with cheerful spirits he had breathed
> The common air; hills, which with vigorous step
> He had so often climbed; which had impressed
> So many incidents upon his mind
> Of hardships, skill or courage, joy or fear;
> Which, like a book, preserved the memory
> Of the dumb animals, whom he had saved,
> Had fed or sheltered, linking to such acts
> The certainty of honourable gain;
> Those fields, those hills—what could they less? had laid
> Strong hold on his affections, were to him
> A pleasurable feeling of blind love,
> The pleasure which there is in life itself.
>
> (65–77)

Though it is a shepherd's life that is described here, this quiet and deeply-felt verse defines the nature of a man's commitment to his existence. It is from the pattern woven between man and his world, from their constant interchange, that life gets its significance. 'The pleasure which there is in life itself' is a 'feeling of blind love' which grows ever stronger as a man binds himself through action to his world. So intense is this commitment that it is unbearable for Michael not to have a son in whom the life can be continued. It is not that the reader merely feels pity for Michael; we feel with him the human need for continuity.

Wordsworth manages the human relationship of husband and wife, father and son, with great sureness. The reason for his success here seems not to be any kind of psychological insight or knowledge of character, but the literary integrity that subordinates the human acts to the vision they embody. The scene of the parting of father and son is moving not because it is natural, but because it combines a series of symbolical and almost ritual acts with the appearance of the natural:

> The Shepherd ended here: and Luke stooped down,
> And, as his Father had requested, laid
> The first stone of the Sheep-fold. At the sight
> The old Man's grief broke from him; to his heart
> He pressed his Son, and kissèd him and wept;
> And to the house together they returned.
>
> (418–23)

The shepherd has ended his admonition with a reference to the grave. It is at this point that the boy stoops down in filial submission, and lays the stone as a token of his commitment to return. Only when the act of submission and commitment has been fulfilled may the old man allow his tenderness to be shown, and then his acts are given a ritual quality by the biblical terms employed; the deliberate formality of 'kissèd him' is no mere casual lapse into archaism, but a stroke of art by which Wordsworth makes the acts of the father and son into formal representative gestures. The final line combines an appearance of great simplicity with the strongest suggestions of united purpose, peace restored, and the pledging of trust; the simple word 'together' in this context gathers to itself all the implications of natural piety developed throughout the poem:

> And to the house together they returned.

The tragedy of the poem does not lie in Michael's death, or in his decay. These are shown as an acceptable part of man's destiny. Michael is not broken by his grief; he continues his work and his vigilance:

> Among the rocks
> He went, and still looked up to sun and cloud,
> And listened to the wind; and, as before,
> Performed all kinds of labour for his sheep,
> And for the land, his small inheritance.
>
> (454–8)

The 'pity which was then in every heart' is not for Michael's personal defeat. It is for the breaking of the link between father and son, for the destruction of the 'natural piety' without which life must lose much of its purpose and value. The loosening of the bond between man and man, so disturbingly described in 'Residence in London', has in this poem affected one of the closest of human bonds, and portends a future of meaninglessness in which man has nothing to strive for. Michael is still strong enough to build the sheepfold, but there is no longer any point in doing so. This poem expresses with wonderful completeness and lucidity the interconnection of man and his world of action, of man with man, and of human hopes and values with the situations in which they are exercised. The son's defection leads to the end of the family, the sequestration of the land, and the darkening of the Evening Star; the interwoven threads of the human pattern have been broken, and the fabric falls apart. In spite of its quietness, 'Michael' expresses a tragic vision compounded of clear perception and a deep concern for human values.

This poem, though Wordsworth says it is 'homely and rude' is of course only so as part of the convention by which all pastoral poetry since Theocritus has proclaimed itself to be artless. A pastoral poem is usually the product of a sophisticated mind, and this is no exception. Wordsworth's triumph in this great poem is to have used the pastoral mode of Theocritus, Virgil, Spenser and Milton, and yet to make the result appear to be simple and natural. Only repeated and careful readings can reveal both how deep the currents of thought and feeling run in this poem, and how masterly is the art by which they are controlled.

7

'RESOLUTION AND INDEPENDENCE'

'Resolution and Independence' was composed by Wordsworth in 1802, but not published until five years later. This is a poem which shows Wordsworth's audacity in taking a most unpromising subject and making it the occasion for one of his profoundest comments on human life, and in particular on the life of a poet. The central figure of the poem is a leech-gatherer Wordsworth and his sister had met with on one of their walks. This deliberate choice of a most unpoetic occupation, and of a most unheroic hero, shows Wordsworth challenging contemporary ideas of decorum and of poetic elevation. Even the modern reader, though we have had more than a century and a half to get accustomed to Wordsworth's boldness, finds himself somewhat disconcerted. For some reason Wordsworth's imagination was aroused by the encounter with this wretched old man, and even the superficially ludicrous nature of the search for leeches did not deter Wordsworth from making this the occasion for one of his most ambitious poems. However, just as the daffodils themselves are not the real subject of 'I wandered lonely as a cloud', so the real subject of 'Resolution and Independence' is not the leech-gatherer himself, but the poet and his fate. Before some explanation of Wordsworth's strange choice of a leech-gatherer as the central figure of the poem can be given, the poem itself must be considered.

The poem begins with a spring morning after a storm. This has raged all night, and left a serene morning:

> There was a roaring in the wind all night;
> The rain came heavily and fell in floods;
> But now the sun is rising calm and bright;
> The birds are singing in the distant woods;
> Over his own sweet voice the Stock-dove broods;
> The Jay makes answer as the Magpie chatters;
> And all the air is filled with pleasant noise of waters.

This beginning expresses the primal joy of existence; the poet rejoices in the beauty he sees around him, a beauty that seems a promise of happiness. This passage resembles the beginning of the Song of Solomon, in which the rain has gone, and the song of the birds announces a season of ecstatic love:

For lo, the winter is past, the rain is over and gone; the flowers appear on the earth; the time of the singing of birds is come, and the voice of the turtle is heard in our land.

(II, 11–12)

The morning is a time of promise; everything speaks of birth, of fertility, and new life:

> All things that love the sun are out of doors;
> The sky rejoices in the morning's birth;
> The grass is bright with rain-drops;—on the moors
> The hare is running races in her mirth;
> And with her feet she from the plashy earth
> Raises a mist; that, glittering in the sun,
> Runs with her all the way, wherever she doth run.

This passage insists on the fertility of nature, on the life which springs from sun and rain and earth, and is expressed in the animal vitality of the hare—a common symbol of fertility—leaping and racing in uncontrolled joy. This description of the perfect harmony and life of nature leads Wordsworth on to consider his own condition; as usual with Wordsworth, he is not concerned with himself as a person, but as a poet. We must regard the questions that he now raises as directed to the life of the imaginative mind. At first the poet is only half conscious of the joy that surrounds him, but it is conveyed to him without his full knowledge and participation, and:

> The pleasant season did my heart employ:
> My old remembrances went from me wholly;
> And all the ways of men, so vain and melancholy.

By so representing the poet's state of mind, Wordsworth reminds us that the ways of men indeed are 'vain and melancholy', and that there is usually a large gap between the harmonious life of nature and a man's own existence. This leads on Wordsworth in the next stanza to a sudden reversal of feeling. The very excess

of joy leads man to a sense of what he has to lose, and therefore
to fear of the future. This is the parable of the Garden of Eden,
in which the knowledge of good and evil separates man from the
natural harmony of the animal kingdom, and compels him to
work and fear for the future.

> But, as it sometimes chanceth, from the might
> Of joy in minds that can no further go,
> As high as we have mounted in delight
> In our dejection do we sink as low;
> To me that morning did it happen so;
> And fears and fancies thick upon me came;
> Dim sadness—and blind thoughts, I knew not, nor could name.

Since the capacity for pain is proportionate to the capacity for
joy, the poet, as a man of 'more than usual organic sensibility',
must experience the extremes of both:

> And fears and fancies thick upon me came;
> Dim sadness—and blind thoughts, I knew not, nor could name.

Though this condition is more keenly felt by the poet, it is of
course common to men, and it is as 'a man speaking to men' that
Wordsworth writes, and not only as a poet speaking for poets.
The nature of man's fears for the future, and of his exile from the
unselfconscious paradise of the hare and the stock-dove, is made
clearer in what follows:

> I heard the sky-lark warbling in the sky;
> And I bethought me of the playful hare:
> Even such a happy Child of earth am I;
> Even as these blissful creatures do I fare;
> Far from the world I walk, and from all care;
> But there may come another day to me—
> Solitude, pain of heart, distress, and poverty.

The poet, more than other men, must if he is to pursue his
vocation avoid being absorbed in 'getting and spending'. Wordsworth regarded the pursuit of gain or worldly ambition as a grave
obstacle to poetic commitment. Yet without care and provision
for the future, the poet is exposed to a fear of 'Solitude, pain of
heart, distress, and poverty'. A commitment to life without 'over-
anxious care' is in one sense a necessary part of the poet's task;

but it brings with it a dilemma for, as Wordsworth suggests here, he has no right to expect others to care for him if he is unable to care for himself. This leads in stanza VII to a consideration of other poets, in particular Chatterton, 'the marvellous Boy', and Burns, who died young and poor, and to the fear that perhaps to be a poet is to be condemned to misery and defeat:

> By our own spirits are we deified:
> We Poets in our youth begin in gladness;
> But thereof come in the end despondency
>   and madness.

So far the poem has led Wordsworth from the height of joy to the very depths of a depression that is not merely momentary, but comes from the contradiction between the poet's capacity for suffering, and the necessity of not being unmanned by the demands of an ordinary existence. It is at this point that Wordsworth suggests that a message is sent to him from 'above'. He does not so much meet the leech-gatherer as become suddenly conscious of the old man before his eyes. It is as though the leech-gatherer is a visitant from another world, suddenly materializing before the gaze of the poet:

> Now, whether it were by peculiar grace,
> A leading from above, a something given,
> Yet it befell that, in this lonely place,
> When I with these untoward thoughts had striven,
> Beside a pool bare to the eye of heaven
> I saw a Man before me unawares:
> The oldest man he seemed that ever wore grey hairs.

Wordsworth with great skill has avoided any obtruding of the oddity of the leech-gatherer at this point. There is a suggestion of loneliness, of the pool 'bare to the eye of heaven', of the silent appearance of the 'Man', without any warning, and finally of his great old age:

> The oldest man he seemed that ever wore grey hairs.

All these suggestions combine to give a visionary quality to the poet's experience. In the next stanza, in a passage which Words-worth himself has explained at some length, the old man is compared with a huge stone which lies on the top of a bald hill, causing all observers to wonder how he came to be there. This association of the old man with a stone gives him an elemental dignity, as though he were part of the universe, rather than merely another member of the human race. This suggestion of the old man as emerging from the total pattern of the universe is carried further in the second part of the stanza, where he is described as being

> Like a sea-beast crawled forth, that on a shelf
> Of rock or sand reposeth, there to sun itself.

We have seen that the poet experiences with the sharpness of pain the sense of his own separateness from the joyful harmony of the natural kingdom. The old man, for all his apparent wretchedness, feels no such separation. He appears when we first meet him as emergent from the rock, and from the animal kingdom, and as still closely linked with them. Wordsworth now describes the man more directly:

> Such seemed this Man, not all alive nor dead,
> Nor all asleep—in his extreme old age:
> His body was bent double, feet and head
> Coming together in life's pilgrimage;
> As if some dire constraint of pain, or rage
> Of sickness felt by him in times long past,
> A more than human weight upon his frame had cast.

This moving passage reminds us that the old man, although he is in a way a part of nature itself, is not thereby exempted from the burden of suffering. On the contrary he has been subjected to the full weight of the natural law, and to everything that 'pain, or rage Of sickness' can do. The effect of this intensely described burden of suffering is to increase our sense of wonder at the old man's powers of resistance, since the forces of nature have cast upon him 'a more than human weight'. Wordsworth next describes the old man more directly. He can do so more safely now, since the sense of mystery and awe has been aroused. The old man is motionless, propped upon 'a long grey staff of shaven wood' which itself suggests the bareness and poverty of his existence. He seems also to be locked up within himself, unaware of the life around him, and as though grown into a state of insensibility that is close to that of the stone which he resembles:

> Motionless as a cloud the old Man stood,
> That heareth not the loud winds when they call:
> And moveth all together, if it move at all.

When the old man moves, he stirs the pond with his staff and:

> fixedly did look
> Upon the muddy water, which he conned,
> As if he had been reading in a book.

The effect of the description of the old man as praeternaturally linked with the universe, as infinitely old, and as bearing an unequalled burden of suffering, gives to the leech-gatherer's stirring of the waters, and looking into them as though 'reading in a book', the suggestion of a diviner, a seer, or a prophet. And indeed this is what Wordsworth turns him into: the leech-gatherer is a sooth-sayer who reveals to the poet the truth about himself and his life. The most difficult part of Wordsworth's task in this poem is to deal with the conversational trivialities which the poet exchanges with the leech-gatherer. If the poem is carelessly read, there seems to be a slightly ludicrous contrast between the appearance and sufferings of the old man and the greeting which the poet now addresses to him: 'This morning gives us promise of a glorious day.' However, this question is not so commonplace as it may appear. The morning has already given to the poet this promise, but it was short-lived, and was followed by the fear that the morning on the contrary gave warning of a very painful and difficult day, and of a painful and almost unbearable future for the poet. In other words, the poet approaches the leech-gatherer, not with a merely commonplace greeting, but with a half-stated question: 'What does the future hold for me?' The old man gives, as we are told, a courteous answer, but the poet is not satisfied, and enquires about the old man's occupation. There is here an implied linking of the poet's occupation and that of the leech-gatherer. The leech-gatherer gives an answer, but before he does so Wordsworth records the sudden illumination of his eyes:

> Ere he replied, a flash of mild surprise
> Broke from the sable orbs of his yet-vivid eyes.

The sudden life displayed in the vivid eyes of the old man suggests a spiritual vitality strangely at odds with the apparent insensibility and near-deadness of his physical frame. Once again the suggestion is of an almost supernatural being, who speaks with the voice of the universe to the questioning poet.

What follows in the next two stanzas is a description of the solemnity of the leech-gatherer's 'lofty utterance', and an account of his wandering from moor to moor to find the leeches which are increasingly hard to come by. The subject-matter, the finding of leeches, may seem somewhat at odds here with the 'lofty utterance'. However, the poet is interested in an occupation which subjects the old man to endless hardship, and offers him only slight hope of reward. He finds it hard to understand how the leech-gatherer can accept such a fate; it is as though a poet were to spend a lifetime of suffering and find few occasions for making genuine poems. Once the parallel between the finding of leeches and the making of poems is understood, the intensity of the interest in the search ceases to be absurd.

The poem now returns to an intenser mode of feeling and thought:

> My former thoughts returned: the fear that kills;
> And hope that is unwilling to be fed;
> Cold, pain, and labour, and all fleshly ills;
> And mighty Poets in their misery dead.
> —Perplexed, and longing to be comforted,
> My question eagerly did I renew,
> 'How is it that you live, and what is it you do?'

This passage expresses what must be taken as the central question discussed by the poem—the problem which the poet has in common with all men, that for every increase in his awareness of the world, and of his own situation in it, he must pay an increment of anxiety and pain. The very capacity for joy brings with it 'the fear that kills; And hope that is unwilling to be fed'. The knowledge of good and evil, the capacity to foretell the future, brings with it a sense of all the perils that lie in wait for man, of 'Cold, pain, and labour, and all fleshly ills'. The poet is concerned most of all with 'mighty Poets in their misery dead', but since all men are in some degree poets, all men are faced with the same dilemma. The question is asked on behalf of mankind: 'How is it that you live, and what is it you do?' This is not merely directed towards the economic problems of leech-gathering. In this context, it is a question about fortitude, about resolution and independence. How can any man bear the burden of living when it is associated with consciousness of what the future may bring?

The answer given by the leech-gatherer is cryptic. He merely declares that he has travelled far and wide looking for leeches, and that they have 'dwindled long by slow decay'. The only part of his answer that is relevant to the poet's question is his insistence that, though the leeches are now hard to find, he still perseveres, and finds them where he can. This answer, although it seems totally inadequate to the problem that troubles the poet, in fact appears to be sufficient. The strange appearance of the old man, his stately and dignified speech, and his quiet acceptance of the burden laid upon him, have combined to admonish and upbraid the poet. The old man ceases to be merely a leech-gatherer, and becomes instead an image of the human task, of commitment to consciousness, to the endless search for what is to be found, no matter what pain may be involved, or what the price to be paid:

> While he was talking thus, the lonely place,
> The old Man's shape, and speech—all troubled me:
> In my mind's eye I seemed to see him pace
> About the weary moors continually
> Wandering about alone and silently.

The leech-gatherer then changes the subject, and talks of indifferent matters, which the poet does not trouble to record. But what he says is now of no great importance. The mysterious messenger has, almost without knowing it, delivered his message. The poet finds in the example of the old man an admonition to himself: 'I could have laughed myself to scorn to find In that decrepit Man so firm a mind.' And he concludes with what seems like a solemn affirmation, that with the 'help and stay secure' of

God he will think of the leech-gatherer, and will not be afraid of what lies ahead of him.

Wordsworth then has achieved, in spite of what seemed to be handicaps of subject-matter and style, a poem that remains impressive and deeply moving, in spite of all the ridicule that can be brought against it. The test of an audacious poem is whether or not it succeeds, and 'Resolution and Independence' assuredly does. The achievement is not only in the imaginative facing and overcoming of anxiety (or *Angst* as it is sometimes called today), but in the poetic transformation of a wretched old man who lives by gathering leeches into a visionary figure speaking to the poet's deepest needs. It is not merely that the poet is given a message; he is seen in the act of framing that message from the very appearance of the leech-gatherer, thus performing the poetic task of investing with life and meaning all the objects of sense. In order to do this his mind must, as Coleridge says, 'dissipate and dissolve' the common appearance of things, in order to create them anew in the imagination. So the leech-gatherer's ordinary 'common-sense' appearance is dissolved:

> The old Man still stood talking by my side;
> But now his voice to me was like a stream
> Scarce heard; nor word from word could I divide;
> And the whole body of the Man did seem
> Like one whom I had met with in a dream;
> Or like a man from some far region sent...

The original appearance has finally yielded to the imagination, and the old man has become a mythic figure; the actual leech-gatherer met by Dorothy and William has become Wordsworth's leech-gatherer, a prophetic and mysterious being speaking for the poets of the ages, and for man in his search for fortitude. The cheerfulness shown by the poet at the end is not merely the endurance of failure; it also expresses the confidence that comes from having succeeded. The poetic struggle has this time been won:

> 'God', said I, 'be my help and stay secure;
> I'll think of the Leech-gatherer on the lonely moor!'

97

Like so many of Wordsworth's poems, 'Resolution and Independence' is at once an account of the workings of the imagination,
and an exercise of it. The leech-gatherer, we are given to understand, will be a talisman for the poet, who when in dejection
will always have in the leech-gatherer a useful reminder of his
own ability to transform the most intractable material, and invest
it with 'the consecration, and the poet's dream'.

8

THE 'IMMORTALITY' ODE

The ode, 'Intimations of Immortality', composed in 1802-4, was highly regarded by Wordsworth, but from Coleridge on his critics have both admired and condemned it, sometimes in almost one breath. Not the least of the difficulties raised by this poem is that of deciding what it actually says. The answer to this question must be found in the poem itself, but it may be useful, on this contentious point, to notice what Wordsworth himself had to say, always remembering that the poet in later years may not be an entirely reliable witness to his original intentions. In a letter written in 1814, he says:

The poem rests entirely upon two recollections of childhood, one that of a splendour in the objects of sense which is passed away, and the other an indisposition to bend to the law of death as applying to our particular case. A Reader who has not a vivid recollection of these feelings having existed in his mind cannot understand the poem.

In a later comment Wordsworth tells us that at times when he was a child the world around him seemed at once intensely dream-like and vivid, both unreal and more than real; and that he felt himself to belong to another world. It is on this recollection that the poem is based; and the doctrine of which it makes use is only one of several ways of talking about an experience which many people remember from their own childhood. From this starting-point, the poem examines the whole story of human life as an exile from an earlier and more perfect state. It expresses man's sense of living in a mode of existence that in some sense is foreign to his essential being. In other words, man lives in the world of the senses, and in space and time, with a recurrent feeling that he has known, or at least is capable of knowing, a more perfect state.

This sense that man has of living in a less than perfect condition has been expressed in many myths, among them the story of the Garden of Eden. This story tells us how, through the eating of the fruit of the tree of knowledge of good and evil, man first knows pain, guilt and anxiety. The myth of the Golden Age, recorded in many classical writers, also reflects man's sense that the life which he normally experiences is not the highest that he is capable of, and that somewhere at some time a primal joy has been left behind. Among the literary myths which express this general feeling, the account given by Plato of man's exile from the world of light and of perfect forms has been the most persistent and influential. It is therefore not surprising to find that Wordsworth makes use of this myth, and acknowledges his use of it.

Here we must distinguish between making use of a myth and believing in it as a doctrine. Wordsworth made this distinction very plainly in what he said to Isabella Fenwick late in his life. Rejecting the view that he was here advancing an argument in favour of belief in 'a prior state of existence' he says that he protests against such a conclusion, which has 'given pain to some good and pious persons'. But he adds:

Though the idea is not advanced in revelation there is nothing there to contradict it and the fall of man presents an analogy in its favour. Accordingly, a pre-existent state has entered into the popular creeds of many nations; and among all persons acquainted with classic literature, it is known as an ingredient in the Platonic philosophy.

There need therefore be no great difficulty on this point, although some critics have made heavy weather of it. The poem clearly makes use of the myth that man is born into this world from a pre-existent state of greater perfection and happiness. Moreover, Wordsworth himself adduces 'classic literature' as the source of this myth, and regards it as commonplace amongst all persons acquainted with this literature. The intention of the poem, as both Coleridge and Wordsworth tell us, is, however, not to restate the Platonic myth in verse; it is to illuminate man's experience of his life in this world, and do so in terms which will speak to the common reader. The poem makes use of the myth of pre-existence, but this is not what the poem 'means'.

In one sense, the meaning of the poem is simple. The poet raises the question of the value of life itself, once the primal joy experienced in childhood has gone by. The first four stanzas are given to a statement of the sense of loss felt by the poet when as an adult he can no longer experience the unity of being and sense of illumination he remembers from his childhood. If Wordsworth had left the poem where he broke off for a period of two years, at the end of the fourth stanza, the poem would have been an elegiac lament on the loss of this childhood sense of mystery and of glory. The fourth stanza ends upon a note of loss:

> Whither is fled the visionary gleam?
> Where is it now, the glory and the dream?

The rest of the poem, which Wordsworth added at a later time, is an attempt to come to terms with man's condition once this primal splendour has deserted him. The next four stanzas (V–VIII) make use of the myth of pre-existence, not only to explain what has been described in the first three stanzas—the loss of childhood joy—but also to show how the business of living, of learning, and of coming to terms with the world of the senses, imposes an increasing burden on the soul.

It is here that Wordsworth makes the most direct use of the Platonic myth. The notion that the soul when it enters this world is entering the dark cave of the senses finds an exact parallel in the 'prison-house' in Wordsworth's poem. The description of Nature as a foster-mother, and not the true mother of the soul, and of its attempts to wean man from his recollections of the celestial world, is also closely related to the myth of the cave in Plato.

Plato is, however, not the only source that Wordsworth draws on. If this account of the world is accepted, the consequence to be drawn is that man's life is one long decline from the bright splendour of childhood into 'palsied Age'; in other words man plays throughout his life a series of roles each of which is less satisfactory, until in the end he is reduced to nothingness. The allusion at the end of stanza VII is clearly to the speech of Jacques in *As You Like It*, where man is shown as acting a series of absurd parts until in his last phase he is reduced to mere senility, 'sans teeth, sans eyes, sans taste, sans anything'. Wordsworth's

statement is less brutally direct, but by drawing upon the association with Shakespeare it achieves much the same end:

> The little Actor cons another part;
> Filling from time to time his 'humorous stage'
> With all the Persons, down to palsied Age,
> That Life brings with her in her equipage;
>   As if his whole vocation
>   Were endless imitation.

What the child is innocently enacting in his play is a grim commitment to a fate which all men have to undergo.

It is this passage that introduces the praise of the child as a
'best Philosopher' and as one who not only reads 'the eternal
mind' but also knows the truths which 'we are seeking all our
lives to find'. Here too the life of the senses is characterized as
'In darkness lost, the darkness of the grave'. The apparent
extravagance of this idea, which was severely castigated by
Coleridge, is less extreme if we remember that the child is here
being contrasted with the adult, and that the child is called a
philosopher only by a kind of paradox. Although 'deaf and silent'
and therefore incapable of understanding what it knows, the child
is a 'philosopher' only by being naturally close to the source of
joy. The terms that Wordsworth uses make it plain that he does
not think of the child as a practitioner of conscious wisdom but as
experiencing the life to which the philosopher aspires. The
praise of the child, moreover, looks less extravagant if it is contrasted with the life which the adult is condemned to live. But the
child's 'philosophy' does not preserve it, in spite of its closeness to
a better world, from the fate of the 'prison-house'. The child is
only too ready to assume the burden of the world:

> Why with such earnest pains dost thou provoke
> The years to bring the inevitable yoke,
> Thus blindly with thy blessedness at strife?
> Full soon thy Soul shall have her earthly freight,
> And custom lie upon thee with a weight,
> Heavy as frost, and deep almost as life!

Some critics have commented adversely on the rhetorical and
strained tone of this passage. Perhaps this verdict does not

sufficiently take account of the irony with which the whole passage is suffused. If Wordsworth were quite solemnly and without reservations addressing the child as a philosopher, and asserting that it knew the truths that all men are looking for, this would be extravagant. But the whole passage is shot through with irony. The child is paradoxically at once the bearer of the heavenly message of joy, and at the same time the willing and even eager agent of its own imprisonment in the world of the senses.

So far the answer given by the poem to the question which it so insistently raises, of the value of the life men live, has been almost entirely a facing of an unpleasant truth, in which a quiet irony is the only defence the poet has against the pain of recognition. With the beginning of the next stanza, however, Wordsworth takes stock of what remains for man to take delight in. There is first of all the memory of childhood, which is not to be valued merely because it is a memory of days of delight, but on the contrary because it causes him to question the absolute value of the world around him. What he values are

> those obstinate questionings
> Of sense and outward things,
> Fallings from us, vanishings;
> Blank misgivings of a Creature
> Moving about in worlds not realised,
> High instincts before which our mortal Nature
> Did tremble like a guilty Thing surprised.

These 'shadowy recollections' are, says the poet, 'the fountain-light of all our day'. These have the power to sustain us in the world of darkness because they give us glimpses of another reality, which, even though we cannot attain it, offers a hope that our lives, however pointless and aimless they may seem, have yet a relationship to a deeply hidden but permanent source of joy:

> truths that wake,
> To perish never:
> Which neither listlessness, nor mad endeavour,
> Nor Man nor Boy,
> Nor all that is at enmity with joy,
> Can utterly abolish or destroy!

The thought of this stanza is therefore complex. It begins by asserting the gratitude of the poet for the childhood sense of unity of being. Even though this is lost, its very existence in the past is a reminder to us that man is more than the sum total of his anxieties, transient pleasures, and petty aims.

So it may be said that the contemplation of childhood has led Wordsworth to a clearer sense of the nothingness of human existence, and from this sense of nothingness he is rescued by the recollection of childhood itself, which remains as testimony to the potentiality of man's nature. This has something of the quality of a religious affirmation. We need not suppose it to be Christian, or Platonic, or to be attached to any particular set of beliefs. All it affirms is that man is sustained in his sense of the futility and pointlessness of the world by a belief that this life of the senses has ultimately some relationship to the totality of the universe. Though far removed from childhood, we can look back and see ourselves as children on the shores of immortality, and be reminded that all men, however far they may travel from it, are still linked with an ultimate reality:

> Hence in a season of calm weather
>   Though inland far we be,
> Our Souls have sight of that immortal sea
>   Which brought us hither,
>   Can in a moment travel thither,
> And see the Children sport upon the shore,
> And hear the mighty waters rolling evermore.

What is stated here is not merely that we can remember our childhood condition. For Wordsworth, the 'child is father of the man', and there is a child within each of us. In 'a season of calm weather', when contemplation can do its work, the mind can conquer time, and 'in a moment travel' to the condition of childhood, not to enter into it, but at least to observe it as immediately before the eye of the mind. The last two lines of the stanza evoke a vivid impression of children playing on the shore with the roar of the ocean around them. The 'recollection' is an imaginative return, not a faded photograph preserved in the memory. This imaginative return to the unity of being of the child is an act that can be deliberately achieved. Childhood, though in one sense left behind, is not lost; its kingdom of heaven is always within us, and may be recovered. This passage is therefore crucial, and marks the turning-point of the thought.

The next stanza (x) returns to the theme of the primal joy, but it is not a mere echo of the earlier passage. The differences must be carefully noted if the poem is to be understood:

> Then sing, ye Birds, sing, sing a joyous song!
>   And let the young Lambs bound
>   As to the tabor's sound!
> We in thought will join your throng,
>   Ye that pipe and ye that play,
>   Ye that through your hearts today
> Feel the gladness of the May!

This passage repeats, with a difference, the language of stanza III, in which the poet's attempt to enter fully into the joy of the natural world was crossed by a 'thought of grief', and in which he asserts, in spite of doubts and feelings of loss, his determination not to allow himself to be separated from that joy. In stanzas III and IV this affirmation is somewhat forced; it is a mere refusal to be exiled from the natural world:

> My heart is at your festival,
>   My head hath its coronal,
> The fulness of your bliss, I feel—I feel it all.

This refusal to be 'sullen' is not firmly based, and it is followed by a statement of the loss which cannot be forgotten:

> Whither is fled the visionary gleam?
> Where is it now, the glory and the dream?

The first four stanzas, then, are not a complete poem, for they contain an unresolved tension. The ode as a whole resolves this opposition, and when the theme of the birds and the lambs is returned to, the aspiration is no longer for a full emotional participation in the life of the natural world, but only for the kind of intellectual sympathy made possible by the insight achieved:

> We *in thought* will join your throng,
>   Ye that pipe and ye that play,

Ye that through *your hearts* today
Feel the gladness of the May!

The poet no longer tries to 'feel' the 'fulness' of the bliss of childhood; it is only the young and innocent who can feel this in their hearts. 'In thought' only is participation possible. The primal joy is left behind, and in its place is left a strengthened faith in the value of all life, and a renewed confidence in the power of intellect to offer support to man in the years that bring 'the philosophic mind'. This intellectual insight is that by which, in stanzas VIII and IX, Wordsworth perceives that what has been lost in childhood may be regarded as in itself a guarantee of man's relationship to a greater world. If this is so, then 'human suffering' may be borne because it is not merely pointless. The poet may then find consolation in all that reminds him of man's condition:

> Though nothing can bring back the hour
> Of splendour in the grass, of glory in the flower;
>   We will grieve not, rather find
>   Strength in what remains behind;
> In the primal sympathy
> Which having been must ever be;
> In the soothing thoughts that spring
> Out of human suffering;
>   In the faith that looks through death,
> In years that bring the philosophic mind.

As though Wordsworth has now come to terms with his own existence, and provided some kind of solution to the anguished question raised throughout the earlier part of the poem, he now turns calmly to the appearances of nature, to 'Fountains, Meadows, Hills and Groves'. He has turned his mind from them to deal with more disturbing topics, but now that the questioning of the value of life has been to some degree settled, he can return to a quieter and deeper enjoyment of the pleasure he finds in the beauty of this world:

> And O, ye Fountains, Meadows, Hills, and Groves,
> Forebode not any severing of our loves!
> Yet in my heart of hearts I feel your might;
> I only have relinquished one delight

> To live beneath your more habitual sway.
> I love the Brooks which down their channels fret,
> Even more than when I tripped lightly as they;
> The innocent brightness of a new-born Day
> > Is lovely yet;
> The Clouds that gather round the setting sun
> Do take a sober colouring from an eye
> That hath kept watch o'er man's mortality;
> Another race hath been, and other palms are won.
> Thanks to the human heart by which we live,
> Thanks to its tenderness, its joys, and fears,
> To me the meanest flower that blows can give
> Thoughts that do often lie too deep for tears.

In turning to the natural world once again, Wordsworth resumes his more habitual quietness of phrasing and a more contemplative poetic mode. He has in this poem reconciled himself with the human condition, and is content, now that he sees that it is not essentially pointless, to accept life on the terms it offers. It is perhaps characteristic of Wordsworth that his highest flight of imagination ends in the re-affirmation of a quiet sanity. Part of this sanity consists in the recognition that after all the adult is a better philosopher than the child. Since he is more intelligent, more experienced, and more fully aware of his nature, he is capable of a deeper love and a fuller appreciation of the world:

> I love the Brooks which down their channels fret,
> Even more than when I tripped lightly as they;
> The innocent brightness of a new-born Day
> > Is lovely yet;
> The Clouds that gather round the setting sun
> Do take a sober colouring from an eye
> That hath kept watch o'er man's mortality.

There is also a sense of profound satisfaction, as at a victory won. 'Another race hath been, and other palms are won.' The tone of refreshment and of new confidence is akin to that of Milton when at the end of 'Lycidas' he turns to new tasks:

> At last he rose, and twitched his mantle blue,
> Tomorrow to fresh woods, and pastures new.

It now remains to consider, not only what the poem means, but

how far it succeeds as poetry. Those who especially value Wordsworth's characteristic quietness must recognize that here he is
achieving something rather different—an unusual energy and
vitality which transforms his verse into a hymn of praise to the
universe, and a celebration of man's place in it. There is an
insistent dance-like beat in the rhythms even of those passages
where Wordsworth is describing the loss of the childhood
radiance:

> There was a time when meadow, grove, and stream,
> The earth, and every common sight,
>> To me did seem
>> Apparelled in celestial light,
> The glory and the freshness of a dream.
> It is not now as it hath been of yore;—
>> Turn wheresoe'er I may,
>> By night or day,
> The things which I have seen I now can see no more.

What has disconcerted some readers is the apparent contradiction between the vitality of the rhythms here and the somewhat
gloomy statement that is being made. This, however, is part of the
intended poetic effect; the remembered glory of the world of
childhood suffuses the poem with joy and life even although the
poet himself feels excluded from that world. This almost magical
reflection of the beauty of the natural world is intensified further
in the second stanza:

> The Rainbow comes and goes,
> And lovely is the Rose,
> The Moon doth with delight
> Look round her when the heavens are bare,
>> Waters on a starry night
>> Are beautiful and fair;
> The sunshine is a glorious birth;
> But yet I know, where'er I go,
> That there hath past away a glory from the earth.

Here the rainbow, the rose, the moon, the waters, and the sunshine form a pattern that is not merely decorative. The rainbow
and the rose are both the complex products of the primal forces of
sunshine, water and earth, while the moon and the stars evoke

the universal framework within which the vital processes are completed. It is by a natural transition that Wordsworth passes from the contemplation of the complexities of the physical world, in the rainbow, and of the world of organic botanical life in the rose, to the vitality of the animal kingdom, and then to himself as a human being in the midst of the creative world:

> Now, while the birds thus sing a joyous song,
>   And while the young lambs bound
>   As to the tabor's sound,
> To me alone there came a thought of grief:
> A timely utterance gave that thought relief,
>   And I again am strong.

The 'timely utterance' seems to have been the poem on the rainbow, three lines of which were prefixed to the poem in 1815:

> The Child is father of the Man;
> And I could wish my days to be
> Bound each to each by natural piety.

This short poem partially achieves the insight attained in the 'Immortality' Ode—an insight which leads the poet to see that he has not in fact lost as a man what was revealed to him as a child—the sense of the ultimate unity of the universe. This affirmation, however, though it reminds us how a poet characteristically deals with his moments of depression, is not enough to sustain him permanently or to enable him to share directly in the joy of the animal kingdom and of the 'happy Shepherd-boy'. In this stanza the 'jollity' is observed from without, in spite of the attempt to enter fully into it. The whole passage is coloured with a sense of the difference between the beauty and joy of the universe and man's capacity to enter fully into and share the joy. In stanzas IV, V, VI, VII and VIII, as we have seen, the poet is concerned with the loss of the primal joy, and the verse is more discursive and shows less poetic intensity. In return, it has for the attentive reader overtones of rueful irony and of quiet humour which it will not do to neglect. The picture of the child at play appears sentimental, but in fact presents a picture of the family happily approving of the child's eagerness to enter the 'prison-house':

> Behold the Child among his new-born blisses,
> A six years' Darling of a pigmy size!
> See, where 'mid work of his own hand he lies,
> Fretted by sallies of his mother's kisses,
> With light upon him from his father's eyes!
> See, at his feet, some little plan or chart,
> Some fragment from his dream of human life,
> Shaped by himself with newly-learned art.

This domestic scene is the prelude to the 'dialogues of business, love, or strife' which will begin the child's progress 'down to palsied Age'. The irony in the stanza that follows is grimmer, for it deals with the subjugation of the soul to the 'earthly freight' of custom. Here Wordsworth achieves a shift of tone to a deeper seriousness:

> Full soon thy Soul shall have her earthly freight,
> And custom lie upon thee with a weight,
> Heavy as frost, and deep almost as life!

Here the imagery of weight, of frost, and of burial, reinforced by the heavy rhythm falling upon the long vowels, achieves an intensity of feeling entirely appropriate to the theme of the poem. The contrast between these lines and the joyous vitality of other passages should remind us of the wide range of poetic power that Wordsworth exhibits in this ode.

In the last stanzas of the poem there is no opposition between the beauty of the universe and man's capacity for joy. These have now been reconciled, and the verse reflects, in its joyful but measured movements, the poet's new-found unity of feeling. Here the organ-stops are opened:

> Our Souls have sight of that immortal sea
> Which brought us hither,
> Can in a moment travel thither,
> And see the Children sport upon the shore,
> And hear the mighty waters rolling evermore.

As we have seen, the final stanza shows a quiet modulating of the music to a peaceful close. Of this poem, and of this poem only when Wordsworth is in question, one is tempted to speak in terms of music, and in particular of the symphonic music of Beethoven.

In range of feeling, in the dramatic shifts in theme and rhythm, and in its expression of the primal grief and primal joy, it seems natural to think of it as symphonic. It must not be forgotten, however, that poetry is never the same as music, and that the ode is not merely a musical outpouring. It is an act of mind, in which what is actually said in the words is an integral part of the total effect.

The movement of mind followed by Wordsworth in the poem may briefly be indicated by the change from stanza IV, in which

> The Pansy at my feet
> Doth the same tale repeat:
> Whither is fled the visionary gleam?

The pansy is the flower of thought (*pensée*); here it prompts the thought of lost joy and of exile from the primal unity of feeling. At the end of the poem, however, Wordsworth has learned to value 'the philosophic mind' as an acceptable recompense for the lost radiance of childhood. He does not claim that 'the philosophic mind' can supply the vital joy of youth. Instead it offers a possibility of a mode of contemplation in which the human emotions are themselves the objects of thought, and form the materials of a vision which compels the imagination, so that pain and grief may be transcended:

> Thanks to the human heart by which we live,
> Thanks to its tenderness, its joys, and fears,
> To me the meanest flower that blows can give
> Thoughts that do often lie too deep for tears.

'Other palms are won'; the joys of childhood give place to the poet's delight in the observing and celebrating of life in all its aspects. The 'meanest flower' is the occasion, not for tears, but on the contrary for '*thoughts*' that are 'too deep for tears'. This line aptly describes the best of Wordsworth's poetry, to which we are never tempted to respond with a lachrymose indulgence of feeling. There is a world of difference between this and Tennyson's

> Tears, idle tears, I know not what they mean.

The difference is between thought and language bewildered by emotion, and emotion 'recollected in tranquillity', and ordered by the imagination into a pattern of intellectual delight. Not only the pansy, but the very meanest flower—the daisy or the buttercup— is for the poet the flower of thought, and capable of flashing like the daffodils on the 'inward eye' as part of a unified vision of the world.

9

'THE PRELUDE' I

No introduction to Wordsworth would be complete without some account of *The Prelude*, but it is impossible in a short book to give more than a general account of its structure and theme, and to look closely at a few representative passages to illustrate its quality. This long poem was written as a part only of a even longer philosophical poem, to be called *The Recluse*. Of this only two parts were completed—*The Excursion* and *The Prelude*. Wordsworth published *The Excursion* in 1814, but although it was completed by 1805 *The Prelude* was not published until after Wordsworth's death. In the Preface to *The Excursion* he says of *The Prelude*:

The preparatory poem is biographical, and conducts the history of the Author's mind to the point when he was emboldened to hope that his faculties were sufficiently matured for entering upon the arduous labour which he had proposed to himself.

This autobiographical poem gives an account of the poet's childhood, youth, and early manhood; but it cannot be adequately understood as merely the story of Wordsworth's life. It is designed also as an account of the growth of the imagination, and incidents in Wordsworth's life that are not relevant to this account—the story of his association with Annette Vallon, for example—are passed over lightly or omitted. The reader should not expect to find in this poem a frank account of Wordsworth's personal life; it is the life of his poetic personality that is recorded.

This is made clear from the beginning, when the poet invokes the breeze—a traditional symbol of inspiration—and seeks for a theme:

> O there is blessing in this gentle breeze,
> A visitant that while it fans my cheek
> Doth seem half-conscious of the joy it brings
> From the green fields, and from yon azure sky.
>
> (I, 1–4)

The breeze blows from nature, but also from heaven itself.

> What dwelling shall receive me? In what vale
> Shall be my harbour? underneath what grove
> Shall I take up my home? and what clear stream
> Shall with its murmur lull me into rest?
> The earth is all before me...
>
> (I, 10–14)

The vale, the grove and the clear stream are not to be understood as parts of the English countryside; they are the landscape of the imagination, akin to the vale of Tempe, the grove of Apollo and the stream of Peneus. In the whole of this introductory passage Wordsworth, by the cadences of his verse and by slight but unmistakeable touches of allusion, shows that he is conscious of following in the steps of Milton, who in his own invocation to his Muse declares:

> Yet not the more
> Cease I to wander where the Muses haunt
> Clear spring, or shady grove, or sunny hill,
> Smit with the love of sacred song.

So Wordsworth, preparing himself like Milton for his task, reminds us of the last lines of *Paradise Lost*:

> The world was all before them, where to choose,
> Their place of rest, and Providence their guide.

Wordsworth, choosing his own dwelling-place of the mind, and his own poetic direction, echoes Milton's words with evident deliberation:

> The earth is all before me.
>
> (I, 14)

And he declares that even if his guide is 'but a wandering cloud' he cannot miss his way. The life he has chosen is one of 'ease and undisturbed delight'—but the liberty he enjoys would be useless without the poetic gift:

> Dear Liberty! Yet what would it avail
> But for a gift that consecrates the joy?
> For I, methought, while the sweet breath of heaven
> Was blowing on my body, felt within

> A correspondent breeze, that gently moved
> With quickening virtue, but is now become
> A tempest, a redundant energy,
> Vexing its own creation.
>
> (I, 31–8)

The breeze of inspiration from without serves to rouse the intellectual energies of the poet's own mind. It is a breeze of spring, which will break up a 'long-continued frost' and enable the poet's mind to grow and blossom.

This then is Wordsworth's invocation to his Muses, thinly disguised as an ordinary and natural account of his situation. The echoes of Milton and of the classical invocation are not mere unconscious recollections; still less are they literary embroidery. The purpose of these allusions is to make it clear that the theme of the poem is not simply the life of Mr William Wordsworth. It is with the life of a poet that *The Prelude* is concerned, and with Wordsworth only as one in the succession of poets who have worked at the common task. It is possible to read the poem as the story of 'Wordsworth the man', but only if the reader ignores or dismisses the insistent reminders that *The Prelude* is written within the tradition of Western poetry, and that it is about the poet as poet, and not as an individual person. This is not to say that the poet has no new tasks. The theme of *The Prelude* is the loss of the paradise of childhood, and of the regaining of that paradise through the power of the developed imagination. Wordsworth is conscious of attempting for his own age what Milton did for his; in an age of science, however, the challenge to the imagination is a new one. It is not in the heavens, but in the human mind itself that he must seek for the source of joy and power. For this reason *The Prelude* is a psychological poem, in the sense that it deals with the 'vital soul' of the poet, the inner resources on which he can draw in his task of giving significance to man's life. So we find Wordsworth making an inventory of these resources:

> When, as becomes a man who would prepare
> For such an arduous work, I through myself
> Make rigorous inquisition, the report
> Is often cheering; for I neither seem

> To lack that first great gift, the vital soul,
> Nor general Truths, which are themselves a sort
> Of Elements and Agents, Under-powers,
> Subordinate helpers of the living mind:
> Nor am I naked of external things,
> Forms, images, nor numerous other aids
> Of less regard.
>
> (I, 146–56)

Where Milton could call on nymphs, dryads, angels, and gods, Wordsworth has only the 'Under-powers' of his own mental equipment. The transformation of the world has to be undertaken by the poet's mind without the aid of the traditional poetic machinery, or of the traditional myths and beliefs. *The Prelude* is designed as the first great poem of an age of science and of scepticism; its aim, however, is not scientific realism, but the assertion of the primacy of man's creative powers.

In describing the growth of the power of imagination, by which the world is given order and significance, Wordsworth asserts the capacity of life to emerge from dead and unorganized matter, and to produce human consciousness itself:

> Dust as we are, the immortal spirit grows
> Like harmony in music; there is a dark
> Inscrutable workmanship which reconciles
> Discordant elements, makes them cling together
> In one society. How strange that all
> The terrors, pains, and early miseries,
> Regrets, vexations, lassitudes interfused
> Within my mind, should e'er have borne a part,
> And that a needful part, in making up
> The calm existence that is mine when I
> Am worthy of myself!
>
> (I, 340–50)

Human consciousness is produced by a harmonizing of opposites; however simple the primary laws of nature appear, they work together in complex ways to create life and the human mind. The mystery which was seen by earlier poets as supernatural is still a mystery, but it is now that of the 'inscrutable workmanship' by which apparently blind forces produce living and conscious beings. *The Prelude*, in telling the history of one mind, recounts the emergence of a human consciousness to what, for Wordsworth, was the highest level it could attain—that of the poet.

The introduction ends with the poet ranging over the past in search of a theme—

> some old
> Romantic theme by Milton left unsung.
>
> (I, 168-9)

Finally he is left with his 'best and favorite aspiration':

> some philosophic song
> Of Truth that cherishes our daily life;
> With meditations passionate from deep
> Recesses in man's heart, immortal verse
> Thoughtfully fitted to the Orphean lyre.
>
> (I, 229-33)

Destiny of the Sate of the soul [handwritten annotation]

This provides a good definition of Wordsworth's aim in *The Prelude*. It is to be a philosophic exploration of the truth of daily life and of the deep recesses of the heart; but this is not to be mere psychological realism. The aspiration is as bold as Milton's—to write 'immortal verse' that is 'fitted to the Orphean lyre'. It is, however, to be 'thoughtfully' fitted—an expression suggesting that the Orphean ecstasy is to be combined with a cool and deliberate intelligence. Coleridge called this 'an Orphic tale indeed', and the poem is Orphic in the traditional sense of dealing with the fate of the soul. When Milton turns to the theme of Heaven and Paradise he says he has written of Hell

> With other notes than to the Orphean lyre.

The 'Orphean lyre' celebrates the soul's ascent, as in the myth of Orpheus and Eurydice, from the darkness of 'Chaos and eternal Night'; Wordsworth's aspiration is to follow Orpheus and Milton, and

> to venture down
> The dark descent, and up to re-ascend,
> Though hard and rare.

The introduction to *The Prelude* ends with a brief account of the paradisal state of childhood, described as a golden age of radiance and spontaneous life (I, 288-300):

117

> Oh, many a time have I, a five year's child,
> In a small mill-race severed from his stream,
> Made one long bathing of a summer's day;
> Basked in the sun, and plunged and basked again
> Alternate, all a summer's day, or scoured
> The sandy fields, leaping through flowery groves
> Of yellow ragwort; or when rock and hill,
> The woods, and distant Skiddaw's lofty height,
> Were bronzed with deepest radiance, stood alone
> Beneath the sky, as if I had been born
> On Indian plains, and from my mother's hut
> Had run abroad in wantonness, to sport
> A naked savage, in the thunder shower.

The details here seem commonplace enough. The child, however, is shown as undergoing the baptism of sun and water in a nature in which he feels utterly secure, a nature bathed in radiance and golden light, where even the 'yellow ragwort' forms 'flowery groves', and the child is naked and unafraid in the thunder-shower. How this state of innocent joy is lost, and how it may with the help of the imagination be largely restored, is the theme of *The Prelude*.

The introduction in Book I leads immediately into the account of childhood and school-time, and from the five-year-old child to the boy of ten; the soul that has been implanted in the world begins to put down roots and to grow under the influence of the 'inscrutable workmanship' which reconciles 'discordant elements':

> Fair seed-time had my soul, and I grew up
> Fostered alike by beauty and by fear.
>
> (I, 301–2)

Beauty and fear dominate the poet's boyhood; joy and guilt are inseparable. While snaring birds or robbing nests the boy experiences exultation and terror:

> and when the deed was done
> I heard among the solitary hills
> Low breathings coming after me, and sounds
> Of undistinguishable motion, steps
> Almost as silent as the turf they trod.
>
> (I, 321–5)

The 'inscrutable workmanship' is busy forming a human mind, weaving its patterns of feelings and perceptions. The innocent fearlessness and joy of the infant is left behind. The process is most fully described in the account of the 'act of stealth' by which the boy takes a boat he finds on the lake and rows off in it. As he rows from the land, the boy is transported to a world of fancy:

> She was an elfin pinnace; lustily
> I dipped my oars into the silent lake,
> And, as I rose upon the stroke, my boat
> Went heaving through the water like a swan.
>
> (I, 373–6)

This passage combines the boy's transformation of the boat into an 'elfin pinnace' with a vivid representation of the physical facts. The physical act of rowing is enacted to the rhythms, and the 'poetic' comparison of the boat with a swan is given unusual truth by making it go 'heaving through the water' in the way swans do move, with a series of powerful strokes. These two modes of experience—that of fact and that of fancy—are modified by the sudden emergence of the boy's guilt, as the mountain towers over him:

> When, from behind that craggy steep till then
> The horizon's bound, a huge peak, black and huge,
> As if with voluntary power instinct
> Upreared its head.
>
> (I, 377–80)

This is an entirely natural event. The highest peak is hidden by the nearer hill, until it is revealed as the boat is rowed from the shore. When this happens, the farther hill seems by an optical illusion to be growing steadily higher. To the boy's guilty mind, the peak seems to be rearing its head; the mountain itself pursues him. Wordsworth shows the boy 'projecting' his own guilt into his surroundings, and by a poetic act natural to childhood, giving a human or super-human life to his surroundings. The interest of this passage is not so much in its 'psychology' as in the account it gives of the beginnings of the poetic consciousness. The boy's terror increases:

I struck and struck again,
And growing still in stature the grim shape
Towered up between me and the stars, and still,
For so it seemed, with purpose of its own
And measured motion like a living thing,
Strode after me.

(I, 380–5)

The experience remains in the boy's mind, transforming the world for him and haunting his dreams; it is from such experiences, Wordsworth suggests, that the poetic imagination is formed. The 'Wisdom and Spirit of the Universe', he says has 'intertwined' for him 'the passions that build up our human soul'. This has been done, 'not in vain'. He has become a poet, since the spirit of the universe has framed his mind

Not with the mean and vulgar works of man,
But with high objects, with enduring things—
With life and nature, purifying thus
The elements of feeling and of thought,
And sanctifying, by such discipline,
Both pain and fear, until we recognize
A grandeur in the beatings of the heart.
Nor was this fellowship vouchsafed to me
With stinted kindness.

(I, 408–16)

Wordsworth's special good fortune, in other words, is that his feelings have been associated from boyhood with 'high objects'— with the permanent and universally interesting mountains, lakes, and streams. His imagination is therefore given a natural language free from the merely temporary complications of the 'vulgar works of man', and therefore always intelligible. The association of the boy's emotions with the very framework of the universe, moreover, gives him a profound confidence in the 'grandeur' of his own nature. In this way a belief in the value of man himself is established. Modern man sometimes feels that he has 'measured out his life with coffee-spoons'. A poet who has measured out his life with mountains, stars, and rivers is less likely to see it as absurd or trivial.

A description of the pleasures of skating follows. It begins with a vivid account of the physical excitement and the happy noise, as the pack of schoolboys hunt along the ice:

> We hissed along the polished ice in games
> Confederate, imitative of the chase
> And woodland pleasures,—the resounding horn,
> The pack loud-chiming, and the hunted hare.
>
> (I, 434–7)

The boy is now living not in the golden age of infancy, but in a later stage in the history of the race; he is re-enacting the existence of man as a tribal hunter. With a stroke of confident art, Wordsworth sets the boyhood activities in a wider context:

> So through the darkness and cold we flew,
> And not a voice was idle; with the din
> Smitten, the precipices rang aloud;
> The leafless trees and every icy crag
> Tinkled like iron.
>
> (I, 438–42)

The sharp echoes from the trees and rocks are like hammer-blows on an anvil in the frozen air; the effect is exactly observed. There is more here than skilful painting of nature; a telling contrast is achieved between the noisy confusion of human voices and the hardness of the enduring and icy crags, which fling back the noise. The suggestion is that the boys in their play are subject to natural laws that are ultimately indifferent to them, and will outlast them. The boys themselves are obscurely aware of this, experiencing the melancholy of the scene even in their play:

> While far distant hills
> Into the tumult sent an alien sound
> Of melancholy not unnoticed, while the stars
> Eastward were sparkling clear, and in the west
> The orange sky of evening died away.
>
> (I, 442–6)

Wordsworth is too subtle an artist to moralize about young life being doomed, or to assert with Gray that 'the little victims play'. He merely sets the skating in the context of the whole earth, and allows the rising of the stars and the setting of the sun to make their comment for him.

Wordsworth, as a boy destined to be a poet, does not remain with the pack, but sets off on his own to pursue the reflection of a star on the ice—a symbolical activity—or to sit and to watch the wheeling of the cliffs about him, a movement partly caused by his own dizziness, and partly by a vision of reality:

> Yet still the solitary cliffs
> Wheeled by me—even as if the earth had rolled
> With visible motion her diurnal round!
> Behind me did they stretch in solemn train,
> Feebler and feebler, and I stood and watched
> Till all was tranquil as a dreamless sleep.
>
> (I, 458–63)

Even here the young poet is pursuing his task; the meditation leads to the appearance of a pattern in the confusion, and to a perception of the ultimate tranquillity in which all life ends. For Wordsworth, a sense of proportion and a sense of perspective are all-important, and he shows himself as acquiring these at an early age.

Book II continues the account of boyhood, and here some of the disadvantages of the elevated Miltonic style begin to show themselves. Even in the quiet and less elaborate style evolved during the eighteenth century, the blank-verse paragraphs with their elaborate syntax and over-running lines are a clumsy instrument for the discussion of commonplace themes. At times Wordsworth avoids absurdity only by a hair's-breadth:

> The garden lay
> Upon a slope surmounted by a plain
> Of a small bowling-green; beneath us stood
> A grove, with gleams of water through the trees
> And over the tree-tops; nor did we want
> Refreshment, strawberries and mellow cream.
>
> (II, 155–60)

This reminds the reader of similar passages in Milton ('No fear lest dinner cool'); the bowling-green and the strawberries and cream have not been given the significance that the style invites us to look for. This is a momentary lapse, and Wordsworth recovers immediately:

But, ere nightfall,
When in our pinnace we returned at leisure
Over the shadowy lake, and to the beach
Of some small island steered our course with one,
The Minstrel of the Troop, and left him there,
And rowed off gently, while he blew his flute
Alone upon the rock—oh, then, the calm
And dead still water lay upon my mind
Even with a weight of pleasure, and the sky,
Never before so beautiful, sank down
Into my heart, and held me like a dream!

(II, 164–74)

This beautifully recreates the world of boyhood, when the mind is always ready to transmute ordinary actions into romance. The boating-party on the lake becomes a little Odyssey, with the discovery of an unknown island. The boy left behind playing his flute on the rock becomes the minstrel of a band of wandering adventurers, his music a celebration of the undisturbed serenity of sky and water. Wordsworth, however, does not lose sight of his theme; the incident is recorded as another stage in the growth of a poet's mind:

Thus were my sympathies enlarged, and thus
Daily the common range of visible things
Grew dear to me.

(II, 175–7)

In this book Wordsworth interrupts his narrative to explain his view of imagination and its place in man's life. The baby, as he tells us, learns from his mother to respond to the beauty of a flower and to the pain and joy of others. By natural piety he learns to become a perceiving mind, and in his turn to share in the creating of a world of value. All men are to some degree capable of living actively within an active universe, responding with imaginative joy to the world of the senses:

Emphatically such a Being lives,
Frail creature as he is, helpless as frail,
An inmate of this active universe.
For feeling has to him imparted power
That through the growing faculties of sense
Doth like an agent of the one great Mind

Create, creator and receiver both,
Working but in alliance with the works
Which it beholds.

(II, 252–60)

All men are therefore poets, and are fully alive and fully human only to the degree to which they have developed this creative power:

Such, verily, is the first
Poetic spirit of our human life,
By uniform control of after years,
In most, abated or suppressed; in some,
Through every change of growth and of decay,
Pre-eminent till death.

(II, 260–4)

At the end of the poem, Wordsworth explains that imagination is necessary to 'intellectual love', and that each man has laid upon him the task of developing his consciousness to the full:

'tis thine,
The prime and vital principle is thine
In the recesses of thy nature, far
From any reach of outward fellowship,
Else is not thine at all.

(XIV, 214–18)

The power of imagination is fostered in the child by society and by nature, but the task of sustaining its growth and of guarding it from the dulling effects of habit is one for each man alone. The poem is not merely egotistical, or merely concerned with the special problems of the poet. For Wordsworth, the poet is 'a man speaking to men', and all men are akin to him in imagination. The poet is no more than a leader, who travels ahead and climbs higher than other men, but only to show them the way.

How the 'poetic spirit' was kindled in the young Wordsworth by his seventeenth year, and how it gave life and value to his world, is described in a later passage in this book:

I felt the sentiment of Being spread
O'er all that moves and all that seemeth still;
O'er all that, lost beyond the reach of thought
And human knowledge, to the human eye

Invisible, yet liveth to the heart;
O'er all that leaps and runs, and shouts and sings,
Or beats the gladsome air; o'er all that glides
Beneath the wave, yea, in the wave itself,
And mighty depth of waters.

(II, 401–9)

The 'sentiment of Being' is an intellectual achievement, arrived at by

> observation of affinities
> In objects where no brotherhood exists
> To passive minds.

(II, 384–6)

These insights, as Wordsworth tells us, become a habit 'deeply rooted' in the mind, and gradually 'steeped in feeling', so that the poet experiences the world with a joyful sense of the complex interconnections of all things, of their vital unity. This is not sentimental enthusiasm, but the delight generated by a powerful intelligence. To think of Wordsworth as inviting us to seek a simple emotional satisfaction from hills and lakes is to misunderstand him radically. The affirmation of the unity of all life in the passage I have just quoted is closer to Newton's praise of the 'great system of the world' than it is to the Victorian cult of nature as a refuge from the pain of consciousness. What unites men, the animals, the birds, and the fish, on the land, in the air, and under the water, is the power of life manifested as movement —as leaping, running, shouting, flying, and swimming. This involves the perception that shouting and singing are modes of movement, that sound is energy, and that life is a pattern of motion unfolded in many different but inter-related rhythms. What man does know of the world is enough to arouse his sense of its wonder and mystery, and to lead him to believe that the vast pattern of life extends beyond his own vision. Wordsworth in this is closer to the natural scientist than he is to those who cultivate the notion of nature as a guide to the simple life. When he invites men to keep alive the poetic spirit, he is asking them to live to the fullest capacity of their intelligence and feelings.

In Book III Wordsworth gives an account of his university days at Cambridge, and in doing so tells us more about the development of his mind. There are touches of dry humour in his account of his new-found independence and manhood:

> My lordly dressing-gown, I pass it by,
> With other signs of manhood that supplied
> The lack of beard.
>
> (III, 40–2)

Wordsworth studied mathematics at Cambridge, and what he writes of Newton must be understood as more than conventional praise. It comes from a respect that is founded in knowledge. From his room in St John's College, the poet looking out sees the statue of Newton in the chapel of Trinity College:

> And from my pillow, looking forth by light
> Of moon or favouring stars, I could behold
> The antechapel where the statue stood
> Of Newton with his prism and silent face,
> The marble index of a mind for ever
> Voyaging through strange seas of Thought, alone.
>
> (III, 58–63)

Newton appears as the great intellectual explorer, and as an example to the poet to seek in his own way for 'universal things', as Newton achieved a universal ordering of the physical world. In his theory of gravitation, which accounted satisfactorily for all observable movements of physical objects on the earth and in the heavens, Newton succeeded in establishing a single unifying principle in events which had seemed disconnected. All finite motions became examples of the gravitational power exerted in proportion to the mass of the objects moved. The imaginations of men were powerfully moved by the new vision of a universe in which, behind all the surface confusions and contradictions, there was after all a clear and demonstrable principle. Wordsworth's aspiration is to achieve in the realm of thought and feeling what Newton achieved in the physical universe:

> Let me dare to speak
> A higher language, say that now I felt
> What independent solaces were mine,
> To mitigate the injurious sway of place

Or circumstance, how far soever changed
In youth, *or* to be changed in manhood's prime.
(III, 99–104)

The power to overcome the changes of place and time is an
intellectual power, like Newton's, which can discover the
universal in what to others appears to be mere accident.

I looked for universal things; perused
The common countenance of earth and sky:
Earth, nowhere unembellished by some trace
Of that first Paradise whence man was driven;
And sky, whose beauty and bounty are expressed
By the proud name she bears—the name of Heaven.
I called on both to teach me what they might;
Or turning the mind in upon herself
Pored, watched, expected, listened, spread my thoughts
And spread them with a wider creeping; felt
Incumbencies more awful, visitings
Of the Upholder of the tranquil soul,
That tolerates the indignities of Time,
And, from the centre of Eternity
All finite motions overruling, lives
In glory immutable.

(III, 109–24)

The search is still for a means of restoring the lost paradise. The
external world—the earth and sky—still show in their harmony
the traces of perfection. It is the inner world of the mind that
awaits its Newton who will reveal the unifying pattern. Wordsworth here is almost scientific in intention; he observes his mind,
'Pored, watched, expected, listened'. This observation gives him
at least a glimpse of a principle within us—he avoids the name of
God, and calls it the 'Upholder'—which provides an ultimate
unity in the mental world, as Newton discovered an ultimate unity
in the physical world. The poet's task is to explore this principle
in himself, and to find a means of bringing it to bear on the objects
that he perceives, so as to transform their appearance of deadness
into a new life and meaning. The process is an intellectual
discipline:

I was mounting now
To such community with highest truth—

127

> A track pursuing, not untrod before,
> From strict analogies by thought supplied
> Or consciousnesses not to be subdued.
>
> (III, 125–9)

Those who think of Wordsworth as an unconscious or emotional poet would do well to note those words. When he talks next of giving a life to stones, he understands very well that the only life they have is that given to them by his imagination:

> To every natural form, rock, fruit or flower,
> Even the loose stones that cover the highway,
> I gave a moral life: I saw them feel,
> Or linked them to some feeling: the great mass
> Lay bedded in a quickening soul, and all
> That I beheld respired with inward meaning.
>
> (III, 130–5)

This is a deliberate process by which the world man lives in is to be redeemed from the deadness to which the physical science of the previous century had consigned it. If the world is not to be full of dead objects, natural forms must be invested with life by the quickening power of the mind. The 'quickening soil' in which the 'great mass' of the physical universe is to grow into life is the soil of the intellect, which by perceiving resemblances everywhere and linking every part of the world with every other gives an organic unity or 'life' to man's experience. Wordsworth was no enemy to science; he feared, however, the acceptance of scientific hypotheses as fixed facts, and the tendency of those influenced by science to see all things 'in disconnection dull and spiritless'. The remedy for this was not a flight from thought, but the more intense application of thought to the whole of man's experience.

Wordsworth insists that this search for a unifying principle was in no sense a 'madness', for he continued to be vigilant in seeking for the differences as well as the resemblances of things. Surveying all things in his experience, he finds there is no resting place for the mind—that his 'bodily eye', as opposed to his 'inward eye', is always active in imposing a logical structure on the world, and keeps his feelings bound 'as in a chain':

An eye

Which from a tree, a stone, a withered leaf,
To the broad ocean and the azure heavens
Spangled with kindred multitudes of stars,
Could find no surface where its power might sleep;
Which spake perpetual logic to my soul,
And by an unrelenting agency
Did bind my feelings even as in a chain.

(III, 162–9)

In Book IV, with his imagination strengthened and developed, Wordsworth returns to his home as to a paradise he has left behind:

With exultation, at my feet I saw
Lake, islands, promontories, gleaming bays,
A universe of Nature's fairest forms
Proudly revealed with instantaneous burst,
Magnificent, and beautiful, and gay.

(IV, 7–11)

The ferryman who takes him across the river appears as 'the Charon of the flood' and suggests a transportation into another world. There is, however, no resting-place in this world of his lost childhood. The valley of his childhood shows signs of change and decay:

'Twas not indifferent to my youthful mind
To mark some sheltering bower or sunny nook,
Where an old man had used to sit alone,
Now vacant.

(IV, 200–3)

Children have grown up, and young girls have lost their beauty. Though he observes the life of the valley with a new interest, he experiences a 'pensive feeling' from the 'shadings of mortality'. The valley is seen as shadowed by death. With this there goes 'an inner falling off'; the young poet seeks distraction in 'a swarm of heady schemes', in 'feast and dance'. The book ends with the appearance of a figure commonplace enough, but given a visionary quality—a soldier met with in the moonlight on a solitary walk:

A more meagre man

Was never seen before by night or day.

> Long were his arms, pallid his hands; his mouth
> Looked ghastly in the moonlight: from behind,
> A milestone propped him; I could also ken
> That he was clothed in military garb,
> Though faded, yet entire.
>
> (IV, 393–9)

A brief quotation cannot do justice to the mysterious and visionary quality of the experience as Wordsworth describes it. The 'ghostly figure' accompanies the poet, and, as they journey on, answers his questions about the hardships he has undergone.

> Solemn and sublime
> He might have seemed, but that in all he said
> There was a strange half-absence, as of one
> Knowing too well the importance of his theme,
> But feeling it no longer.
>
> (IV, 441–5)

Wordsworth makes of the soldier met with in the moonlight an admonitory figure, like the leech-gatherer. His life of hardship and service is one the poet must imitate; he too must know 'the importance of his theme' and have the strength to pursue it, even though the task is painful. This strength is achieved through detachment, through learning to 'care and not to care'. The figure of the soldier plays the same part in *The Prelude*, coming at a crisis in the young poet's life, as does the 'familiar compound ghost' that appears to the poet in *The Four Quartets*. As they part, the poet looks back:

> And so we parted. Back I cast a look,
> And lingered near the door a little space,
> Then sought with quiet heart my distant home.
>
> (IV, 467–9)

The note of quiet determination indicates a renewed faith in the poet's task and a new confidence in his own strength. The last line of the book also recalls the last words of *Paradise Regained*:

> He unobserved
> Home to his mother's house private returned.

Both Christ in Milton's poem, and the poet in Wordsworth's, have had their dedication tested and confirmed.

10

'THE PRELUDE' II

Book v is simply entitled 'Books', but the theme is nothing less than the example of intellectual exploration offered by great writers and thinkers. To this point, writes Wordsworth, he has been concerned chiefly with 'the speaking face of heaven and earth' as his 'prime teacher'. He is now to deal with the work of man's intellect:

> Thou also, man! hast wrought,
> For commerce of thy nature with herself
> Things that aspire to unconquerable life;
> And yet we feel—we cannot choose but feel—
> That they must perish.
>
> (v, 18–22)

There follows a deeply felt passage in which the poet laments the perishable nature of even the greatest works of man's intellect, and longs for 'an element' on which the mind might stamp an imperishable mark. The thought of the vulnerability of art and science to the ravages of time is followed by another visionary experience like that with the old soldier. This time it is a dream of an Arab who shows the poet a stone—representing Euclid, and the knowledge given by mathematics and science. He also holds a shell representing poetry and vision. The poet hears in this shell, when he puts it to his ear, a prophecy of final destruction to all the works of man. The Arab rides away on his dromedary, the poet in his dream mysteriously 'keeping pace' with him. The Arab is merged in the poet's mind with Don Quixote, and the dream ends with a great flood of waters gathering upon the Arab, who rides off on his 'unwieldy creature' with the symbols of science and of poetry 'still in his grasp'. The poet wakes in terror, and sees the book he has been reading lying by his side.

The dream is told as Chaucer might have told it, with a touch of humour mixed with its seriousness. The Arab who is also a

Don Quixote is bound on an 'enterprize' to bury the two 'books' represented by the stone and the shell, to save them from the flood. The task of the intellectual mounted on his own unwieldy steed of the human mind, is also to preserve science and poetry from the flood of destruction which seems always to gather head. The identifying of the Arab with Don Quixote suggests that this may be a tilting at windmills, an attempt like that of Canute to hold back the sea. But Don Quixote is also a positive ideal, the hero of commitment even when commitment seems hopeless and foolish to others. The Arab as a 'demi-Quixote' is by no means to be pitied; this commitment to what seems to be a certain defeat is the permanent condition of the adventurous human intellect:

> Nor have I pitied him, but rather felt
> Reverence was due to a being thus employed;
> And thought that, in the blind and awful lair
> Of such a madness, reason did lie couched.
>
> (v, 149–52)

There are enough people in the world, Wordsworth continues, to 'take in charge their wives, their children'; he himself wishes for the strength to imitate 'that maniac's fond anxiety' and go on 'like errand':

> Oftentimes at least
> Me hath such strong entrancement overcome,
> When I have held a volume in my hand,
> Poor earthly casket of immortal verse,
> Shakespeare, or Milton, labourers divine!
>
> (v, 161–5)

The total commitment that great works of intellect require seems like a madness incompatible with an ordinary settled existence. Wordsworth in the long run chose a settled existence, the life rather than the work, and with that choice left the heroic poetic task behind him. He was not, in the end, a Don Quixote.

The rest of the book is concerned with a defence of imaginative literature in the education of children, and tells us little about Wordsworth's own reading, and that in general terms. The book ends, however, with a strong affirmation of the world of poetry as a source of 'knowledge' and joy:

                              Visionary power
        Attends the motions of the viewless winds
        Embodied in the mystery of words:
        There, darkness makes abode, and all the host
        Of shadowy things work endless changes,—there,
        As in a mansion like their proper home,
        Even forms and substances are circumfused
        By that transparent veil with light divine,
        And, through the turnings intricate of verse,
        Present themselves as objects recognized,
        In flashes, and with glory not their own.
                                        (V, 595–605)

The work of 'mighty Poets', then, creates a second nature in which
the objects seen in the world are transformed and illuminated.
The radiance of which Wordsworth speaks here is that which
he has found in the daffodils when they are transformed by the
perceiving mind, and when later they 'flash' upon the 'inward
eye'. The objects of experience, thus transformed, become the
symbolic expression of the 'visionary power' which the poet
communicates to the world. This offers us a brief account of the
poetry of *The Prelude*. The incidents taken from the real life of
Wordsworth are, as we have seen, invested, as part of a myth of
the rediscovery of paradise, with a significance that they did not
possess in themselves.

   Book VI deals further with Cambridge, and in particular with
Wordsworth's love of geometry. This he represents as characteristic of poets, who will always seek for a refuge from the
teeming fertility of their own minds in the 'clear synthesis built up
aloft' by the mathematician. This love of mathematics is not un-
connected with the central passage of this book. Leaving Cambridge, the poet travels to the Alps, and is confronted with a
scene of terrible grandeur:

                         The immeasurable height
        Of woods decaying, never to be decayed,
        The stationary blasts of waterfalls,
        And in the narrow rent at every turn
        Winds thwarting winds, bewildered and forlorn,

The torrents shooting from the clear blue sky,
The rocks that muttered close upon our ears,
Black drizzling crags that spake by the way-side
As if a voice were in them, the sick sight
And giddy prospect of the raving stream,
The unfettered clouds and region of the Heavens,
Tumult and peace, the darkness and the light—

(VI, 624–35)

The passage begins by proclaiming the height of the mountains
as 'immeasurable'; it is a sight that baffles human measurement.
The scene resists the imagination, as London later resists it;
bafflement and frustration combine with fear, giddiness, and
sickness in a terror that is both physical and mental. The poet
who turned to mathematics as a refuge from an inner turmoil
finds himself confronted with the outer turmoil of an unfamiliar
nature. He achieves a provisional ordering of the scene in terms
of its grandeur and terror, and a faith that its confusions can
somehow ultimately be seen, if only by God, as a kind of
harmony; all the confusions he describes are

like the workings of one mind, the features
Of the same face, blossoms upon one tree;
Characters of the great Apocalypse,
The types and symbols of Eternity,
Of first, and last, and midst, and without end.

(VI, 636–40)

The magnificent rhetoric with its biblical implications goes
with what is essentially a religious affirmation. The ultimate
harmony is not attainable by man; the vision of nature at its most
terrible and destructive is not one that Wordsworth feels he must
himself pursue. Wordsworth's greatness finds its limitation in his
unwillingness to confront the ultimately chaotic and destructive
forces; he was not destined to write the equivalent of *King Lear*.

In Book VII Wordsworth, recounting his period of residence in
London, presents an image of the city as Hell. He begins his
account with a picture of London as he hoped in his 'simple faith'
to experience it—a heaven of delight to which he eagerly looked
forward:

> I then had heard
> Of your green groves, and wilderness of lamps
> Dimming the stars, and fireworks magical,
> And gorgeous ladies, under splendid domes,
> Floating in dance, or warbling high in air
> The songs of spirits!
>
> (VII, 121–6)

With a dramatic shift in the next paragraph Wordsworth addresses himself to the real city as he knows it:

> Rise up, thou monstrous ant-hill on the plain
> Of a too busy world!
>
> (VII, 149–50)

This 'monstrous ant-hill' is a world of confusion and din, where everything is bewildering, and where even the ordering minds of 'Boyle, Shakespeare, Newton' are mixed inextricably with the reputation of 'some quack-doctor':

> Thy every-day appearance, as it strikes—
> With wonder heightened, or sublimed by awe—
> On strangers, of all ages; the quick dance
> Of colours, lights, and forms; the deafening din;
> The comers and the goers face to face,
> Face after face; the string of dazzling wares,
> Shop after shop, with symbols, blazoned names,
> And all the tradesman's honours overhead:
> Here, fronts of houses, like a title-page,
> With letters huge inscribed from top to toe,
> Stationed above the door, like guardian saints;
> There, allegoric shapes, female or male,
> Of physiognomies of real men,
> Land-warriors, kings, or admirals of the sea,
> Boyle, Shakespeare, Newton, or the attractive head
> Of some quack-doctor, famous in his day.
>
> (VII, 152–67)

London presents to the poet's senses a phantasmagoria in which the confusion and disharmony rise to the shrill pitch of the 'female vendor's scream'—a bedlam from which he escapes gratefully into any quiet corner that offers a prospect of order and peace:

> A raree-show is here,
> With children gathered round; another street
> Presents a company of dancing dogs,

> Or dromedary, with an antic pair
> Of monkeys on his back; a minstrel band
> Of Savoyards; or, single and alone,
> An English ballad-singer. Private courts,
> Gloomy as coffins, and unsightly lanes
> Thrilled by some female vendor's scream, belike
> The very shrillest of all London cries,
> May then entangle our impatient steps;
> Conducted through those labyrinths, unawares,
> To privileged regions and inviolate,
> Where from their airy lodges studious lawyers
> Look out on waters, walks, and gardens green.
>
> (VII, 174–88)

This is no merely superficial criticism of the town or a confession of the poet's personal inability to enjoy it. The city is presented, not only as disorderly, lacking in real connection between man and man, and superficial, but also as cruel or indifferent. Moreover, everything in the city is false and imitative. The world of art is one of empty shows, in which painting and music are linked with

> giants and dwarfs,
> Clowns, conjurors, posture-masters, harlequins.
>
> (VII, 271–2)

Wordsworth describes the city only as its life is reflected in the outward shows of the theatre, the law courts with their 'brawls of lawyers', the pulpits, where the 'comely bachelor' expresses himself in affectation and absurdity. This is a world of:

> Folly, vice,
> Extravagance in gesture, mien, and dress,
> And all the strife of singularity,
> Lies to the ear, and lies to every sense.
>
> (VII, 578–81)

In the midst of the crowd there appears a figure representative of the human condition—a blind beggar whose identity is known only by a label on his chest—an image as Wordsworth tells us of man's ignorance of himself and of the world around him. This moving appearance of the blind beggar in the midst of the folly and lies of the city is a telling comment on the world that Wordsworth is here describing. Modern man on his 'monstrous ant-hill' has lost his human identity:

> Amid the moving pageant, I was smitten
> Abruptly, with the view (a sight not rare)
> Of a blind Beggar, who, with upright face,
> Stood, propped against a wall, upon his chest
> Wearing a written paper, to explain
> His story, whence he came, and who he was.
> Caught by the spectacle my mind turned round
> As with the might of waters; an apt type
> This label seemed of the utmost we can know,
> Both of ourselves and of the universe;
> And, on the shape of that unmoving man,
> His steadfast face and sightless eyes, I gazed,
> As if admonished from another world.
>
> (VII, 637–49)

In the passage that follows, in which Wordsworth describes the fair of St Bartholomew, the suggestion of a hell on earth is more strongly advanced. There is perhaps something prophetic in Wordsworth's account of a society seeking endlessly for sensation and abandoning its creative intellectual powers. This is a world in which we hear only a feeble voice from those who are essentially strangers to us:

> The feeble salutation from the voice
> Of some unhappy woman, now and then
> Heard as we pass, when no one looks about,
> Nothing is listened to.
>
> (VII, 665–8)

This city in which 'no one looks about, Nothing is listened to' is a world in which men are no longer linked by 'natural piety'. It is also a world of violence and terror:

> What say you, then,
> To times, when half the city shall break out
> Full of one passion, vengeance, rage, or fear?
> To executions, to a street on fire,
> Mobs, riots, or rejoicings?
>
> (VII, 671–5)

St Bartholomew's fair is, as Wordsworth says, the 'true epitome

Of what the mighty City is herself', a world in which 'the whole creative powers of man' are 'asleep'. The fair itself is described in terms that at once look back to the anarchy and darkness of the last passages in Pope's *Dunciad*, and forward to Dickens' London.

> All moveables of wonder, from all parts,
> Are here—Albinos, painted Indians, Dwarfs,
> The Horse of knowledge, and the learned Pig,
> The Stone-eater, the man that swallows fire,
> Giants, Ventriloquists, the Invisible Girl,
> The Bust that speaks and moves its goggling eyes,
> The Wax-work, Clock-work, all the marvellous craft
> Of modern Merlins, Wild Beasts, Puppet-shows,
> All out-o'-the-way, far-fetched, perverted things,
> All freaks of nature, all Promethean thoughts
> Of man, his dulness, madness, and their feats
> All jumbled up together, to compose
> A Parliament of Monsters. Tents and Booths
> Meanwhile, as if the whole were one vast mill,
> Are vomiting, receiving on all sides,
> Men, Women, three-years' Children, Babes in arms.
>
> (VII, 706–21)

Here the city becomes 'one vast mill' which satanically vomits forth men, women, children and babes in arms—human lives caught on the wheel of a machine which threatens their utter destruction, in a world 'barbarian and infernal'.

The city then, is a hell, not only because it is inherently chaotic, mechanical, and inhuman, but also because the poet finds his own imagination threatened and confused by it. It is much harder to achieve here the 'order and relation' which the poet's mind imposed upon the complexities of the valley of the Wye.

> Oh, blank confusion! true epitome
> Of what the mighty City is herself
> To thousands upon thousands of her sons,
> Living amid the same perpetual whirl
> Of trivial objects, melted and reduced
> To one identity, by differences
> That have no law, no meaning, and no end—
> Oppression, under which even highest minds
> Must labour, whence the strongest are not free.
>
> (VII, 722–30)

Even the strongest minds find it difficult to perceive law and meaning in the confusion of such a scene. However, Wordsworth does not wholly despair of imposing some imaginative order on this confusion. He adds that the scene is not wholly 'an unmanageable sight' to the man

> who looks
> In steadiness, who hath among least things
> An under-sense of greatest; sees the parts
> As parts, but with a feeling of the whole.
>
> (VII, 733–6)

It is significant that Wordsworth at this point turns for reassurance to the mountains and the forms of elemental nature to remind him of the ultimate resources of the human intellect. It is in 'the mountain's outline and its steady form' that his belief is refreshed in the powers of the human mind to achieve an ordered vision:

> Like virtue have the forms
> Perennial of the ancient hills; nor less
> The changeful language of their countenances
> Quickens the slumbering mind, and aids the thoughts,
> However multitudinous, to move
> With order and relation.
>
> (VII, 756–61)

So strong are the 'forms' of the poet's past experience that even in the 'vast receptacle' of the town he can achieve an ordering vision:

> The soul of Beauty and enduring Life
> Vouchsafed her inspiration, and diffused,
> Through meagre lines and colours, and the press
> Of self-destroying, transitory things,
> Composure, and ennobling Harmony.
>
> (VII, 767–71)

The description of London given in this book does not at first suggest composure and harmony. There is, however, an important difference between confusion and a poetic representation of confusion. Wordsworth succeeds in transforming the raw chaos of the town into a myth of damnation—a myth which is as much the product of the ordering mind as Dante's Inferno or Milton's Hell.

139

That this was by deliberate intention is shown plainly enough in the account in Book VIII of a second visit to London, when the city appears to Wordsworth as awful in its grandeur. It has been given a mythic quality by the power of imagination, and he now enters it like a traveller

> who, from open day,
> Hath passed with torches into some huge cave,
> The grotto of Antiparos, or the Den,
> In old time haunted by that Danish Witch,
> Yordas; he looks around and sees the vault,
> Widening on all sides.
>
> (VIII, 560–5)

The merely chaotic inferno now appears as a place of shifting lights and darkness, where spectres appear and disappear. The resemblance to the literary hells in Homer, Virgil, Dante, and Milton is evident; and the passage ends with a scene that is meant to remind us of the damned souls in Dante:

> there the shape
> Of some gigantic warrior clad in mail,
> The ghostly semblance of a hooded monk,
> Veiled nun, or pilgrim resting on his staff:
> Strange congregation! yet not slow to meet
> Eyes that perceive through minds that can inspire.
>
> (VIII, 584–9)

The last line here is of great interest. Even the chaos of London may be transformed by the imagination into a significant order. The 'Eyes that perceive' must, however, do so 'through minds that can inspire'. It is with the help of the poetic tradition, and of his great predecessors, that Wordsworth constructs a human vision of a scene that at first appeared to be merely a confusion. With the help of Dante and Milton, London may be experienced as a part of human history—

> chronicle at once
> And burial-place of passions, and their home
> Imperial, their chief living residence.
>
> (VIII, 594–6)

In Book VIII Wordsworth, turning from the hell of London,

compares it with the life of the people of his own valley, who live by farming and by a simple commerce. Their 'rustic fair', in which there is 'only here and there a stranger' is a festival of life, where 'gaiety and cheerfulness prevail'. The account is meant to serve not as a guide to the tourist in the Lake District, but as an image of what life ought to be. This is a world of 'rural peace',

> tract more exquisitely fair
> Than that famed paradise of ten thousand trees,
> Or Gehol's matchless gardens.
>
> (VIII, 75–7)

This true paradise is one that man may inhabit if he wishes—a world that exceeds in delight all the enchanted gardens of the fancy. After evoking famous gardens of delight and 'domes of pleasure' he asserts:

> But lovelier far than this, the paradise
> Where I was reared.
>
> (VIII, 98–9)

This world, however, is not untouched by sorrow:

> But images of danger and distress,
> Man suffering among awful Powers and Forms;
> Of this I heard, and saw enough to make
> Imagination restless.
>
> (VIII, 164–7)

He therefore still feels the need to sing of human pain and suffering, and in the meantime rejoices that his imagination has been nourished by the harmonies of nature and the undistorted life of men in the quiet valley. The whole book is a retrospect in which Wordsworth takes stock of his progress, and of how far a concern for 'human-kind' has replaced his earlier love for the purer forms of nature. The question is now an important one, for he has been repelled by the life of London, and is about to face the challenge of the French Revolution, in which men sought by political action to create a paradise on earth.

The account of his residence in France shows Wordsworth confronted for the first time with the world of action. He is drawn to the ideals of the revolution, but disenchanted by the tyranny it gives rise to. Worst of all, he is betrayed into disloyalty to his own country. His love affair with Annette Vallon is indirectly recounted, as a nightmare story of failure and madness.

> Into a deep wood
> He fled, to shun the haunts of human kind;
> There dwelt, weakened in spirit more and more;
> Nor could the voice of Freedom, which through France
> Full speedily resounded, public hope,
> Or personal memory of his own worst wrongs,
> Rouse him; but, hidden in those gloomy shades,
> His days he wasted,—an imbecile mind.
>
> (IX, 578–85)

This is of course not a direct portrait of the poet; but it gives an indication of the severe intellectual and moral crisis that occupies the whole of Books IX and X. The world of action, and even the world of thought, seem to have betrayed him:

> This was the crisis of that strong disease,
> This the soul's last and lowest ebb: I drooped,
> Deeming our blessed reason of least use
> Where wanted most.
>
> (XI, 306–9)

From this crisis he is saved, as he says, by his sister, who through her love

> preserved me still
> A Poet, made me seek beneath that name,
> And that alone, my office upon earth.
>
> (XI, 346–8)

The failure of the world of action, and Wordsworth's own failure in it, mean, however, that he must seek a poetic task which frees him from that world. What that task is we are told in the books with which *The Prelude* ends.

At the end of Book IX Wordsworth takes his farewell of the hope of an earthly paradise offered by the French Revolution, and turns instead to a different ideal—the achievement of a 'great society' of human minds:

There is
One great society alone on earth:
The noble Living and the noble Dead.

(XI, 394–6)

The great minds of the past are to be the 'ladder' by which the spirit may

reascend
To health and joy and pure contentedness.

(XI, 397–8)

The true paradise is in the mind, and in the power of the mind to transform what it observes. With this world of action is left behind—the world that is celebrated in the *Aeneid* and in *Paradise Lost*—and the pastoral poet Theocritus is invoked; turning to Sicily and its idyllic poetry, Wordsworth writes:

Child of the mountains, among shepherds reared,
Ere yet familiar with the classic page,
I learned to dream of Sicily: and lo,
The gloom, that, but a moment past, was deepened
At thy command, at her command gives way;
A pleasant promise, wafted from her shores,
Comes o'er my heart: in fancy I behold
Her seas yet smiling, her once happy vales...

(XI, 424–31)

The passage is addressed to the exiled Coleridge, but its relevance to Wordsworth's own situation is plain. At the beginning of the next book he declares that 'human ignorance and guilt' have 'detained us'; we have been 'compelled to look' on 'spectacles of woe' and human error.

Not with these began
Our song, and not with these our song must end.—

(XII, 7–8)

If man's condition is to be improved, the human mind itself must be nourished with joy; and his world must be transformed by his own imagination. So Wordsworth returns to the world of nature as it is irradiated by the human mind:

The morning shines,
Nor heedeth Man's perverseness; Spring returns,—

143

> I saw the Spring return, and could rejoice,
> In common with the children of her love,
> Piping on boughs, or sporting on fresh fields,
> Or boldly seeking pleasure nearer heaven
> On wings that navigate cerulean skies.
>
> (XII, 31–7)

If, then, the sources of human joy are in the human mind, the task of the poet is to free the imagination from the chains of habit in which it is imprisoned. For this task the poet was prepared in earlier life, as he has shown:

> I had known
> Too forcibly, too early in my life,
> Visitings of imaginative power
> For this to last: I shook the habit off
> Entirely and for ever, and again
> In Nature's presence stood, as now I stand,
> A sensitive being, a *creative* soul.
>
> (XII, 201–7)

The transformation of experience by what the mind brings to it is illustrated by the experience of being lost on the moors and seeing a gibbet on which a murderer had been hung in iron chains, and a girl carrying a pitcher on her head.

> It was, in truth,
> An ordinary sight; but I should need
> Colours and words that are unknown to man,
> To paint the visionary dreariness
> Which, while I looked all round for my lost guide,
> Invested moorland waste, and naked pool,
> The beacon crowning the lone eminence,
> The female and her garments vexed and tossed
> By the strong wind.
>
> (XII, 253–61)

The 'visionary dreariness' is as much a part of the poetic imagination as the radiance that is cast on other objects. Although Wordsworth does not tell us into what patterns of the mind the beacon, the gibbet, the pool, and the girl are fitted, it is evident that they are the elements of a tragic vision, linked with past reading and past experience, and capable of being used as the starting point of a poem. The poetic spirit is not concerned to make the world appear beautiful, but to make it intensely interesting. When Wordsworth talks, as he does so often, of the power of Nature to communicate with men, he is not speaking of any 'ordinary sight', of trees and rocks as we habitually see them. His 'Nature' is a world where 'rocks, and stones, and trees' are transformed by the imagination into significant and even symbolical objects. The world of nature is a world of thought, in the creation of which the individual mind is not acting alone, but with the aid of all the other minds that have modified man's view of his world:

> The genius of the Poet hence
> May boldly make his way among mankind
> Wherever Nature leads; that he hath stood
> By Nature's side among the men of old,
> And so shall stand for ever.
>
> (XIII, 295–9)

Nature is the creation of all human imaginations, and it is the poet's task to join in the endless renewal of man's vision of the world by the 'great society' of scientists and poets. Book XIII, therefore, ends fittingly with a vision of the Druids as teachers, performing their magic transformations:

> Long-bearded teachers, with white wands
> Uplifted, pointing to the starry sky,
> Alternately, and plain below, while breath
> Of music swayed their motions, and the waste
> Rejoiced with them and me in those sweet sounds.
>
> (XIII, 345–9)

In the concluding book (XIV) Wordsworth recounts the ascent of Snowdon. The first book began with the poet asking what 'vale' is to receive him. The seventh ended with the 'infernal' scenes of the city. At the beginning of the eighth book, the poet addresses Helvellyn, the mountain that stands above the valley of his childhood:

> What sounds are those, Helvellyn, that are heard
> Up to thy summit, through the depth of air

> Ascending, as if distance had the power
> To make the sound more audible?
>
> (VIII, 1–4)

The invocation of the mountain at the half-way point of the poet's journey is a preparation for the ascent of Snowdon in the last book. This is made, by careful selection of detail, into a symbolical ascent. Led by 'a trusty guide' the poet and his friend set out to see the sun rise from the top of Snowdon. Their path is through fog and mist; as they climb, they are deep in meditation, broken only by the barking of the shepherd's dog in search of a hedgehog. The travellers struggle against the pull of the earth:

> With forehead bent
> Earthward, as if in opposition set
> Against an enemy, I panted up
> With eager pace, and no less eager thoughts.
>
> (XIV, 28–31)

Now the ground begins to brighten, and

> a light upon the turf,
> Fell like a flash.
>
> (XIV, 39–40)

This is, however, not the sun, but the moon that shines out radiantly as the climbers emerge from the mist, and the whole panorama of cloud appears below, with the 'ethereal vault' of the stars now visible overhead. Moreover, through a gap in the clouds they look down to the earth below:

> A fixed, abysmal, gloomy, breathing-place—
> Mounted the roar of waters, torrents, streams
> Innumerable, roaring with one voice!
>
> (XIV, 58–60)

That this is not to be understood as only the story of an actual expedition, but as a significant part of the poet's story, is made plain:

> When into air had partially dissolved
> That vision, given to spirits of the night

> And three chance human wanderers, in calm thought
> Reflected, it appeared to me the type
> Of a majestic intellect, its acts
> And its possessions, what it has and craves,
> What in itself it is, and would become.
>
> (XIV, 63–9)

The vision of the moonlight illuminating the world becomes

> the emblem of a mind
> That feeds upon infinity, that broods
> Over the vast abyss, intent to hear
> Its voices issuing forth to silent light
> In one continuous stream.
>
> (XIV, 70–4)

The creative power of the human mind, itself a part of the divine creative power, is imagination, which, as Wordsworth says, is 'Reason in her most exalted mood'. This power links the poets with 'the Deity', and makes them into powers, or underagents, of the divine will:

> Such minds are truly from the Deity,
> For they are Powers; and hence the highest bliss
> That flesh can know is theirs—the consciousness
> Of Whom they are, habitually infused
> Through every image and through every thought,
> And all affections by communion raised
> From earth to heaven, from human to divine.
>
> (XIV, 112–18)

The ascent of the mountain is made in this way to represent the ascent of the human imagination to a god-like state of vision and joy, and even to

> that peace
> Which passeth understanding.
>
> (XIV, 126–7)

The task of poetry is to transform men's lives by transforming their vision of the world, and rescuing them from a 'universe of death'. It is to this task that Wordsworth dedicates himself:

> Prophets of Nature, we to them will speak
> A lasting inspiration, sanctified

By reason, blest by faith: what we have loved,
Others will love, and we will teach them how.
(XIV, 444–7)

Wordsworth in the closing lines of the poem is uncertain whether he will be given the life and power to 'accomplish aught of worth' to justify his giving the 'story of himself' in *The Prelude*. The poem remained unpublished until his death, perhaps because he thought that he had in fact not accomplished the task outlined for the poet in his 'Orphic tale'—to show men the divinity of their own natures.

THE SONNETS

Most of Wordsworth's sonnets—of which there are many—are best understood as public declamation, in which Wordsworth attempts to express a patriotic or pious sentiment as a public representative of the English people. The manner is generally Miltonic, and leaves little room for the intense contemplation characteristic of much of Wordsworth's writing. 'Milton! thou shouldst be living at this hour' (1802) is a good example of this grandly rhetorical and public manner. Wordsworth addresses Milton with some solemnity, and speaks on behalf of England, declaring that the English collectively are 'selfish men'. The penitential note, produced by a time of national danger, merges in the sestet into an image of Milton as a star. This image tells us very little about Milton, but draws its force from the cosmic setting, which Wordsworth handles with his usual sureness:

> Thy soul was like a Star, and dwelt apart;
> Thou hadst a voice whose sound was like the sea:
> Pure as the naked heavens, majestic, free.

The homage to Milton is uncritical and praises him for virtues which he probably did not possess, and which have nothing to do with his greatness:

> So didst thou travel on life's common way,
> In cheerful godliness; and yet thy heart
> The lowliest duties on herself did lay.

Poems of this kind are valued in the degree to which the reader shares the sentiments expressed, and this in itself will change with the times. In time of war the sonnet 'It is not to be thought of', which praises the British love of freedom, awoke a response which it is not likely to evoke in less troubled times. Normally the English reader feels somewhat embarrassed to be informed that 'In every thing we are sprung Of Earth's first blood, have titles manifold'. Much the same may be said of the other patriotic poems, and also of the numerous religious and pious sonnets that Wordsworth wrote in later years. Most of Wordsworth's sonnets, then, must be regarded as inferior to his best work. However, there are a small number that amply repay a close and careful reading.

'Surprised by joy—impatient as the Wind' (1815) is the record of Wordsworth's grief, experienced long after her death, for the loss of his daughter Catherine. We need not concern ourselves with the biographical implications, because this poem, whatever its relationship to Wordsworth's own life, expresses with unusual clearsightedness the experience of separation through death.

The poem begins with a movement of joy and surprise, reflected in the rapid acceleration in the first line and in the first half of the second line, followed by a sudden stop, and with the sense of emptiness evoked by the echoing 'Oh! with whom':

> Surprised by joy—impatient as the Wind
> I turned to share the transport—Oh! with whom
> But Thee, deep buried in the silent tomb,
> That spot which no vicissitude can find?

The hollow sounds of 'Oh! with whom' are echoed by the rhyme of 'tomb', and a slight touch of perfectly controlled irony is added by the reflection that the lost child is now in 'That spot which no vicissitude can find'—in other words, at peace in the grave. As so often in Wordsworth, the experience described is a recovery of lost time, made possible by a particular coincidence of circumstances. But this recovery of lost time is the recovery of pain, and with pain the poet feels guilt, because he has not been faithful in memory to the lost child:

> Love, faithful love, recalled thee to my mind—
> But how could I forget thee? Through what power,
> Even for the least division of an hour,
> Have I been so beguiled as to be blind
> To my most grievous loss!

What is expressed here is the sense of betrayal through even a momentary forgetfulness of the 'grievous loss'. Even the tiniest intervals of the present ought to be filled with memory of the lost child, for otherwise the loss is absolute. The sense of time immediately passing is very exactly given in

> Even for the least division of an hour

where the light stresses and the delicately placed fricatives enact for the reader the passing of minute fractions of time. This sense of time as it is immediately experienced contrasts with the absolute changelessness of 'That spot which no vicissitude can find'. In the sestet the attempt is made to recover the full sense of the moment of extreme grief experienced at the time of bereavement:

> That thought's return
> Was the worst pang that sorrow ever bore,
> Save one, one only, when I stood forlorn,
> Knowing my heart's best treasure was no more;
> That neither present time, nor years unborn
> Could to my sight that heavenly face restore.

The personal grief here is to some degree caught up in and overwhelmed by the poet's perception of the absoluteness of the loss. The rhythms move with a slow and solemn tread, and the echoing open vowels are tolled out like a knell, with the rhyme powerfully aiding. The recovery of the moment of grief in a way represents a triumph over time, for in the intensity of his contemplation the poet achieves a tragic delight. There is, however, no easy consolation or false sentimentality in the poem. The child is gone forever, and 'neither present time, nor years unborn' can restore her to his sight.

The 'Mutability' sonnet (1821), by contrast, deals with the power of time as it is experienced historically, in its effects on ideas and institutions. The opening of the poem likens the process of change to music and describes a scale, or graph, of growth and decay:

> From low to high doth dissolution climb,
> And sink from high to low, along a scale
> Of awful notes, whose concord shall not fail;
> A musical but melancholy chime.

The word 'dissolution' here means both the period of growth and the period of decay, which are seen to be part of a single process. So the life of an institution or an idea, even when mounting to the height of its maturity, is climbing the scale of growth and dissolution, and moving towards its end. This scale of growth provides by an analogy with music a harmony to be heard only by the philosophical listener. It is only by holding the various notes of the scale in the memory, or by hearing them with historical attention, that the 'concord' can be heard. Those who are too deeply involved in the process itself will not perceive the harmony:

> Which they can hear who meddle not with crime,
> Nor avarice, nor over-anxious care.

The poet finds the music 'melancholy', indicating that he speaks with a detachment which enables him to regret, but not to be deeply distressed by, the pattern that he perceives in all human affairs.

This is not merely the language of disillusion, as the next lines make plain:

> Truth fails not; but her outward forms that bear
> The longest date do melt like frosty rime,
> That in the morning whitened hill and plain
> And is no more.

Here a distinction is made between the outward forms of religions, philosophies, and political systems, and the purposes that these systems exist to serve. Each of them may be to some degree the embodiment of truth, but each contains in its structure some falsity which, sooner or later, will bring about its end. The comparison with hoar-frost suggests one of the ways in which ideas and institutions may lose their power, by a gradual yet rapid melting away. The 'rime' that covers hill and plain seems to be universal, yet when we next look it has evaporated in the sun. These lines suggest that the poet is prepared not merely to regret the passing of existing forms, but also to assent to their vanishing as part of a process by which a frozen and superficial falsity is removed.

The worn-out forms of ideas and institutions, however, are also removed by more violent collapse, as in the fall of:

> the tower sublime
> Of yesterday, which royally did wear
> His crown of weeds, but could not even sustain
> Some casual shout that broke the silent air,
> Or the unimaginable touch of Time.

Here the tower with its 'crown of weeds' presents an ironical picture of an institution which proudly displays the signs of its antiquity, while its apparently solid structure is being steadily broken apart by the new life forcing its way through the cracks and joints of the stone. The weeds that seem so unimportant and powerless have in fact the strength to dislocate the stones of which the tower is built. This process of disintegration is invisible but inexorable; the very weight of the tower, by which it has been held together so long, will assist in its sudden collapse when the hidden forces have done their work. The tower may be brought down by 'Some casual shout that broke the silent air'—the slightest vibration being enough, when the undermining forces have reached the point of balance, to bring the whole structure down. The 'casual shout' appears to the observer to be the cause of the collapse of the tower. But the apparent causes of change are not its real causes; they are only the triggers that release forces that have worked out of sight. The sonnet expresses throughout, but especially in the last lines, the idea of time as operating in mysteriously hidden ways, so that man can never fully understand the past, or foretell the future with confidence or with absolute despair. This sonnet succeeds in advancing the idea of inevitable change in history without suggesting that history is determined.

The ideas expressed in the poem are enforced not only by the imagery, but also by the skilful use of rhythm and sound. The echoing phrase 'And is no more' which overflows from the octave into the first line of the sestet, imposes a pause as though of wonder at the silent vanishing of the frost. It is followed, by an abrupt contrast, with the dropping of the tower, so that the apparent difference between the two processes is dramatically brought to the reader's attention. And in the last line a series of light stresses and short vowels compels a quiet reading, and the delicate pattern of the consonants supports the idea of the subtle working of imperceptible forces behind the apparently simple march of events.

The sonnet on Westminster Bridge (1802) records a moment of vision in which Wordsworth for once is able to achieve a satisfactory ordering of the complexities of the city. This is made possible by the silence of the morning and by the poet's freedom from involvement in the labyrinths of the town. From the far side of the river, the city is seen not as merely a confusion of houses, but as a complex scene which can be ordered by the human mind. The first lines record the arousing of the imagination by what lies before the eyes:

> Earth has not anything to show more fair;
> Dull would he be of soul who could pass by
> A sight so touching in its majesty.

In what follows the imagination awakens fully:

> This City now doth, like a garment, wear
> The beauty of the morning; silent, bare,
> Ships, towers, domes, theatres, and temples lie
> Open unto the fields, and to the sky;
> All bright and glittering in the smokeless air.

The city which wears the beauty of the morning 'like a garment' is of course a personification; but it is a personification quite different from those of Gray and Collins. Wordsworth carefully checks the suggestion of the city as a person before it emerges into too precise a picture. The idea of the city as 'wearing' the morning as a garment is allowed to develop only to the point at which we feel the presence of a unifying life. Without this suggestion the list of things which follows would be merely a mechanical catalogue. The 'Ships, towers, domes, theatres, and temples' are seen as individual things, 'All bright and glittering in the smokeless air', and at the same time they are given a profound unity, because they form the garment worn by the city as an organic living thing. Moreover, this image recognizes that the city is a world of many different appearances; and the beauty that it shows at this time, when seen from a particular place, is only one of its many appearances. The word 'now' suggests the past history of the city, and prepares the mind for the images of its distant past, and for a suggestion of the mystery of its future:

> Never did sun more beautifully steep
> In his first splendour, valley, rock, or hill;
> Ne'er saw I, never felt, a calm so deep!
> The river glideth at his own sweet will;
> Dear God! the very houses seem asleep;
> And all that mighty heart is lying still!

The last lines of the poem return to the image of the city as an organic being:

> Dear God! the very houses seem asleep;
> And all that mighty heart is lying still!

The force of these lines lies in the reminder they give us of two different aspects of the scene. The city is a 'mighty heart', and the centre from which the life is spread through the whole nation. At the same time it is a collection of individual persons and families, as we are reminded by 'the very houses seem asleep'. So the city is seen both as the heart of a nation and of its enduring life and at the same time the home of many different families and many different people at a particular point of time. This poem succeeds in uniting an intense sense of the particular time and the particular place with an equally strong sense of the whole historical and geographical pattern which forms its background. The poem ends with a quiet suggestion that the organic life of the city will sooner or later, like all living beings, come to an end.

In the Duddon sonnets (1806–20) Wordsworth follows the course of the River Duddon from its source in the mountains to the sea, providing sonnets appropriate at each stage of the journey, and at the same time following the life of an individual and the life of the nation. The 'native stream' of the first sonnet appears in 'morning light', and in the second sonnet it is hailed as a 'child'. In sonnet XIX the 'struggling rill' has grown into a 'brook of loud and stately march'. In this way, which the reader can easily follow for himself through the whole sonnet sequence, the course of the River Duddon is made significant of more general and serious concerns. A number of the sonnets in this sequence are examples of Wordsworth's contemplative verse at its most subtle and at its most precise. Sonnet XXI, 'Whence that low voice?', is a good example. This poem begins with the low sound of a whisper, suggesting the ghostly thinness of the recollection quietly aroused by the associations of the river:

> Whence that low voice?—A whisper from the heart,
> That told of days long past, when here I roved
> With friends and kindred tenderly beloved;
> Some who had early mandates to depart,
> Yet are allowed to steal my path athwart
> By Duddon's side; once more do we unite,
> Once more beneath the kind Earth's tranquil light;
> And smothered joys into new being start.

The figures of those who have 'departed' appear almost stealthily in the consciousness of the poet; they 'steal my path athwart'; and the verb 'steal' suggests not only the slight touches by which the memory is awakened, but also the furtiveness of the figures which like ghosts now appear before the poet's mind. In the last three lines of the octave the stronger movement and more vigorous pattern of sounds suggests that the ghosts are gaining vitality, becoming more real and immediate, and bringing with them the upwelling of long-forgotten feelings. 'The kind Earth's tranquil light' suggests by ironical opposition the gloomy under-world of past time in which the ghosts of the departed have lingered.

The sestet shows Wordsworth's art at its most assured:

> From her unworthy seat, the cloudy stall
> Of Time, breaks forth triumphant Memory;
> Her glistening tresses bound, yet light and free
> As golden locks of birch, that rise and fall
> On gales that breathe too gently to recall
> Aught of the fading year's inclemency!

This beautiful passage makes use of two images. That of the

goddess-like figure of Memory is made to merge, by a process like that of a 'dissolve' in a film, into the birch trees whose boughs rise and fall gently in the breezes. So the goddess is there, and not there. The natural scene is transformed and yet remains itself. As with the slight personification of the city in the sonnet on Westminster Bridge, the personification of memory is limited, and at no point becomes too precise. The goddess is suggested by her 'glistening tresses' which are immediately identified through the simile with the 'golden locks of birch'. At the same time the thought of the passage is precise. There are occasions when memory breaks out of its imprisonment in the cloudy vagueness of our past experience; when it does so it is 'bound' by the laws of association which determine that a particular scene shall call to our mind events which have been lost in the past. At the same time memory is 'free', in the sense that on such occasions it achieves a triumph over the destructive power of time. The process described is therefore at once natural and yet wonderful, and it gives to those who experience it a sense of the miraculous. The last line has a haunting resonance that is characteristic of Wordsworth's best sonnets. The poem ends with the dying fall of 'the fading year's inclemency'. This evocation of autumn, in the golden locks of the birch trees, carries with it suggestions of fading of life, and with it the sense that the poet himself will in due course become a ghost. This recognition of the power of time is, however, only one of the chords of feeling struck by the poem: the dominant idea is that of the capacity of the human mind, in favourable circumstances, to enjoy at least an occasional respite from the ordinary laws of time.

The Duddon sonnets are worth careful reading not only for their value as individual poems, but as together composing a single longer poem. They lead to three final sonnets in which Wordsworth develops his rhetorical powers in one of their grandest flights. Though these sonnets have the limitations of rhetoric, and may be taken as an attempt on Wordworth's part to assert a confidence in the future and an acceptance of human fate that are not absolutely founded in contemplative perception, they ring truer than most of the political and religious sonnets.

In particular the philosophical acceptance of the historical process, as illustrated by the stream, represents one genuine part of Wordsworth's sensibility. Though one is left with the strong impression that Wordsworth is no longer capable of the complex integrity of his earlier poetry, the rhetoric here testifies to a reconciliation with the historical process, and may be taken as expressing what became a characteristic nineteenth-century view of history:

> Still glides the Stream, and shall for ever glide;
> The Form remains, the Function never dies;
> While we, the brave, the mighty, and the wise,
> We Men, who in our morn of youth defied
> The elements, must vanish;—be it so!
> Enough, if something from our hands have power
> To live, and act, and serve the future hour;
> And if, as toward the silent tomb we go,
> Through love, through hope, and faith's transcendent dower,
> We feel that we are greater than we know.

In this sonnet Wordsworth prefigures the Victorian mode. Although Tennyson could not have achieved quite the strength and firmness of this sonnet, the general pattern of the thought, the sentiment, and the verse would not be out of place in his work. A comparison of this sonnet with his *Ulysses*, for example, will indicate the close affinity.

> There lies the port; the vessel puffs her sail;
> There gloom the dark, broad seas. My mariners,
> Souls that have toiled, and wrought, and thought with me,—
> That ever with a frolic welcome took
> The thunder and the sunshine, and opposed
> Free hearts, free foreheads—you and I are old;
> Old age hath yet his honour and his toil.
> Death closes all; but something ere the end,
> Some work of noble note, may yet be done,
> Not unbecoming men that strove with Gods.

The tone, as in the last sonnet of the Duddon series, is 'heroic'. The manner is public and rhetorical, the sentiment both comfortable and comforting. The vagueness that afflicts Wordsworth's sonnet in the last lines

(Through love, through hope, and faith's transcendent dower
We feel that we are greater than we know)

has in Tennyson become a more habitual way of considering man's situation and prospects. The later Wordsworth, like Tennyson, too often provides 'noble' attitudes, elevating sentiment, and a diluted Miltonic verse that has become a literary manner. After 1820 there is an evident failure of imaginative energy. By this time the great work lay behind him, and Wordsworth offered to a new age a poetry that was content to illustrate the moral ideas of the established Church and the established order. Tennyson and other Victorian poets learned all too well how such poetry is written; if they looked at the younger Wordsworth they saw little of the adventurer

Voyaging through strange seas of thought, alone.

Wordsworth, at the end of *The Prelude*, thanks Coleridge for 'softening down' the 'over-sternness' which had led him to seek

that beauty, which, as Milton sings
Hath terror in it.

As we have seen, much of the early poetry has terror in it. The readiness to look at the destructive forces of the world and record their power over men's lives is an essential part of Wordsworth's genius. With its fading after 1805 Wordsworth became what the Victorians valued him for—an official comforter and reassurer. With the fading of the tragic vision, the power of joy which is its counterpart also vanishes. The later Wordsworth is shrewd, humorous, kindly, and always competent; but it is for the intellectual and moral audacity of the poetry of his earlier years that he is to be valued.

INDEX OF PASSAGES QUOTED